HOW TO
ATTRACT
WILDLIFE
TO YOUR
GARDEN

DAN ROUSE

HOW TO ATTRACT WILDLIFE TO YOUR GARDEN

CONTENTS

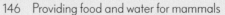

WHY I WELCOME WILDLIFE

We may not see our gardens as a wild space or miniature reserve, but even the smallest area can be transformed for a host of species to enjoy.

My garden is my refuge. When the world gets a bit too much, there's nothing like having lunch outside listening to the birds and watching the squirrels perform their acrobatics trying to reach the feeders. Birds are my true passion, but as I have watched them over the years, I have appreciated more and more that without the many other species involved in the ecosystem, they would not be able to thrive. This goes for all wildlife in a garden and in a much wider area. Everything is interdependent, and it's fascinating to observe and uncover all the connections.

We may think we have to travel to special reserves to see wildlife, but it's possible to get much more intimately acquainted with nature closer to home: in our gardens. I remember as I was growing up being excited to watch the bats hunting around the garden hedges and tree line. Even now, 20 years later, I still get excited and stop everything to watch hedgehogs out in the garden, or look among the flowers to find out which butterflies prefer the flower species that I've planted.

In this book, the first two chapters introduce wildlife that you might find in a garden, and what it needs. The following chapters focus on different types of wildlife: from invertebrates to reptiles and amphibians, birds, and mammals. There is then a final chapter on observing garden wildlife and getting to know it better. I include projects and ideas to implement in your garden, and directories of over 100 common species that may visit.

Wildlife can and will adapt to any given space, so let's share our gardens through the year with wild companions, and enjoy living with the snuffling of mice, the gentle songs of birds, and the buzzing of bees. By making our gardens more of a haven for wildlife, we can make a difference to those species needing extra love and care.

Providing natural food sources such as nectar-rich lavender, and a nesting box for bumblebees, enriches the habitat in your garden.

UNDERSTANDING WILDLIFE

UNDERSTANDING WILDLIFE

The wildlife of a garden can form an incredibly rich and complicated ecosystem, made up of interdependence and interaction. This chapter offers some basic definitions of the types of wildlife you're likely to find in your garden, along with information about when you're likely to see them, and their range of behaviours. Understanding how wild creatures use your garden is a great starting point for taking action to meet their needs.

Foxes visit gardens in cities and rural areas, using them to hunt and forage for food, to breed, and as a refuge.

WHAT COUNTS AS WILDLIFE?

In the broadest sense, wildlife is made up of the living things – birds, mammals, insects, and reptiles, as well as plants – that occur in a place.

In our cities, fields, and hills, the wildlife is clearly very different from that found in other settings, such as African savannahs and the jungles of South America. But every location, including your own garden (however small that may be), contains a range of wildlife that visits and makes its home there. Some species are "native" (they have been part of the wildlife of that area for millennia), while others have been introduced from different parts of the world, deliberately or accidentally – but all make up the local wildlife. Together they form an ecosystem, a community of interacting species. As you get to know the wildlife in your area and garden, you will see how species behave, why they visit or live in your garden, and when certain species are around.

Gardens can offer different benefits to wildlife, from a steady source of food and water, to shelter and a safe place to breed and raise young or to hibernate in the winter. The range of wildlife that can visit a garden over the course of a year is astonishing. Larger creatures, such as foxes, badgers, snakes, and even birds of prey may be rare and exciting to see, but it's possible to find fascination in even the tiniest garden inhabitant, such as a pond skater or centipede.

Residents, migrants, and vagrants

One of the main appeals of wildlife is the fact that it changes throughout the seasons. Many of us mark points in the year by the first swallow we see, or by spotting a familiar butterfly in spring. We notice birds arriving in our gardens to set up for nesting and breeding, and we hear and see pollinators through the spring and summer gathering nectar from our plants, enabling the flowers to set seed and form fruits.

Common species that spend their whole year in a place are known as "resident" species. They breed, feed, and overwinter in the same location. Robins, blue tits, woodlice, bumblebees, and wood mice are all examples of residents that are in the garden all year.

"Migrants" are species that spend a certain amount of time in one area and the rest of the year in another. Some travel from the UK each year to warmer climates to find food during the winter months, returning in spring. Other more northerly species migrate to the UK

Ladybirds are one of our most distinctive insects, seen on plants in summer, and hibernating in winter.

in winter for warmer weather. Migrants include birds such as chiffchaffs and blackcaps, moths such as convolvulus hawk moths and silver Y, butterflies including painted ladies and clouded yellows, and bats such as Nathusius's pipistrelles.

Occasionally you may see a scarce species – usually a bird – that has wandered or been blown off course and out of its usual home range. It's known as a "vagrant" species.

Do plants count as wildlife?

Plants are the pillars of the ecosystem as they make food by combining energy from the sun with moisture and nutrients from the soil. Without plants, all wildlife (and life on Earth) would be lost. They offer nectar and food to pollinators and birds, all-important cover and

Moss is often overlooked as a plant in the garden, but it is a valuable plant for amphibians like this common toad, due to its ability to hold moisture.

water for insects, amphibians, mammals, and birds, and when they decompose they provide nutrients in the soil (see also pp.60–61). Garden plants come in many different forms: flowering plants, shrubs, trees, water plants, mosses, algae, and lichens. While we may introduce many plants ourselves, others will self-seed or arrive in our gardens naturally; think of the dandelions in your lawn or the forget-me-nots that spring up in your borders. For the purposes of this book, we will be discussing and suggesting plants as an essential benefit to other wildlife rather than as wildlife in themselves.

Unwanted wildlife

So-called "pests" come in all forms, from the snail feasting on your precious bedding plants to the night-time visits from the local fox. But if we truly want to support wildlife in our gardens, we have to consider all wildlife – not just the species we like. It helps to think in terms of the garden as its own ecosystem in which all species play a part. If we remove selected species, it can take away part of the food chain (see pp.24–25), making other garden populations, such as birds, less secure. For example, the slugs, snails, and caterpillars that eat their way through seedlings and vegetables are rarely loved by gardeners. But they are valuable food for hedgehogs, amphibians, birds, and others. If we kill off these unwanted invertebrates with pesticides, we're taking away a key source of nutrition for other species – or, even worse, poisoning them with those same chemicals. Accepting the presence of unwanted wildlife often involves a change of mindset, or an adjustment in how you garden. To give a couple of examples:

- Small white butterflies lay their eggs on brassicas such as cabbages and kale, and the caterpillars eat the leaves. It's possible to grow other foodplants, such as nasturtiums, nearby to attract these caterpillars away from the crops. The caterpillars can eat their fill, while also providing food for other wildlife.

- Species that people perceive as risky, like wasps and adders, are often unpopular. But remember: wasps are prolific pollinators, and adders are shy and rarely seen (although spectacular if you do see one), and tend to reserve their venom for their prey. The adder is likely to be passing through, though it's best to keep children and pets away.

In this book, all wildlife is welcome as part of a balanced, thriving garden. The more we know about creatures, loved and traditionally unloved, the more we can appreciate them.

These caterpillars of the large white butterfly (above), along with those of the small white, grow rapidly and feed on the leaves of brassica plants.

Caterpillars are an essential food source for birds, like this great tit. Over 10,000 caterpillars are needed to feed a brood of growing chicks.

DIFFERENT TYPES OF WILDLIFE

Each chapter in this book focuses on a category of wild creatures. These pages offer a glimpse into the amazing range of garden wildlife.

Wildlife can be broadly divided into vertebrates, which are creatures that have a backbone, and invertebrates, which don't. Invertebrates include all insects, snails, worms, and other soil-dwelling creatures, plus some pond creatures. Birds, mammals, reptiles, and amphibians are all vertebrates. Invertebrates tend to be small and numerous in our gardens, while vertebrates are usually larger and therefore rather more noticeable when they pay your garden a visit.

Insects

Insects are invertebrates that have six legs, and often wings. They can live on the ground, or spend much of their lives in the air. Most reproduce by laying eggs. The more insects and invertebrates that are in a garden, the healthier the ecosystem. Some, such as the red soldier beetle (left) eat nectar, pollen, and other insects, while others play an important role in decomposing plant material, as well as providing food for other species.

Pollinators

This group of insects feeds on pollen and nectar. They include some of our most-loved species such as butterflies and moths as well as bees, including the buff-tailed bumblebee (left). As they visit flower heads they pick up pollen from one flower and deposit it on others. This enables pollination to occur, so that the plant can set seed and produce fruit. Pollinators (along with many other species) are often referred to as "beneficial insects". Many of them are in rapid decline for a number of reasons, including the loss of habitat as cities expand and natural spaces are paved over. Pesticides used on crops and in gardens are also a huge problem as they kill the beneficial insects as well as the "pests". Every garden needs to support pollinators.

Other invertebrates

The many other invertebrates are usually small, ground-dwelling creatures. These can include slugs (such as this leopard slug, left) and snails, woodlice, and spiders (arachnids, with eight legs). Invertebrates are the foundation of our garden ecosystems. Many break down organic matter in the soil to release nutrients. They hunt for other invertebrates (including insects), and eat plants, and are in turn food for birds and small mammals. If you have a pond, there are many other pond-dwelling underwater creatures to discover (see pp.108–109).

Reptiles

Secretive creatures, reptiles
are cold-blooded, which means that
they cannot produce their own body
heat. Instead they live in sunny spots
in the garden, gaining warmth and
energy from the sun. There are two main
groups – snakes, such as the grass snake,
and lizards, including the common lizard
(right). Reptiles may sometimes be seen in
gardens, often scuttling in the undergrowth in
search of food, and emerging to bask.

Amphibians

Also cold-blooded, amphibians include
frogs, toads, and newts (left). These
little creatures start life as aquatic
animals, living in water. As they
mature and develop lungs, they
move out onto land, and are
found not only in and near ponds,
but also in boggy or damp areas
of the garden.

Birds

A huge range of bird species visit gardens, from small sparrows and blue tits (right), to medium-sized finches, and larger thrushes and pigeons. It's even possible to see birds of prey, such the sparrowhawk, in a garden. Birds are adaptable and will explore and make use of different items we provide for them. Some birds are in the garden all year round, and these are joined by others that migrate in spring and autumn.

Mammals

The simplest definition of a mammal is a warm-blooded vertebrate that gives birth to live young, though there are exceptions to this. Arguably the most versatile group of animals in the world, mammals vary widely in their appearance, abilities, feeding habits, and more, and occur in all sorts of habitats. In gardens, we can see small mammals such as mice, voles, and shrews, but also larger species such as foxes and badgers (left). Even nocturnal mammals such as bats are very common in gardens, using hedges and plants as hunting grounds for prey.

Diurnal

Many different species are diurnal (active during the day). Reptiles sit and soak up the sun. Nectar is most readily available from plants in the day, and many insects, including bees and butterflies, feed on this nectar. Most birds are also daytime visitors.

Crepuscular

Dawn and dusk is when we may see some wildlife looking for their last feed before sleep or emerging from their daytime slumber. They can become prey for barn owls hunting. Bats emerge to begin their feeding frenzy for the evening, hunting for crepuscular insects.

Great tit

Bats

Peacock butterfly

Brimstone butterfly

Yellow underwing moth

Bumblebee

Tawny owl

Nocturnal

Badgers and foxes are two of the most common nocturnal creatures, along with shrews and mice, which scurry looking for food. Owls such as tawny owls are prolific hunters during the night. Moths fly, looking for night-flowering plants. Amphibians move from one place to another.

Earthworm

Badger

WHEN IS WILDLIFE ACTIVE?

Animals have evolved to take advantage of the conditions at various times of day.

We often have a familiar relationship with creatures that visit our gardens in the day because this is when we are mostly around to see them. But many are crepuscular (active at dawn and dusk), while others are nocturnal (active in the night). Some come out at dusk to escape the heat of the day – amphibians often shelter in the day and move around as darkness falls. Others feed at night to secure a supply of food: moths visit flowers that open at night so they are not competing with day-flying moths and butterflies. Night predators such as owls, bats, and cats have excellent hearing, smell, and night vision so that they can hunt effectively. It's worth taking time to sit quietly as it gets dark to observe the activity around you. You could also set up a camera to capture the action (see p.180–81).

The majority of wildlife is most active in spring and summer when it's warm enough to breed and when food is abundant. In autumn, activity slows down, and in winter many species hibernate, including reptiles, amphibians, and some mammals such as hedgehogs. Some migrant birds (see pp.114–15) arrive in our gardens in autumn from the north to feed on berries and seeds, while summer migrants fly south to warmer regions.

Daytime sees the most activity in the garden, but a different range of creatures emerge in the evening and at night.

WILDLIFE BEHAVIOUR

Although different species show very varied behaviours, the purpose behind them is often shared.

To attract wildlife to your garden it helps to understand how different species behave, and the reasons for their behaviour, so that you can aim to meet some of their needs. Behaviour falls into four main categories: the search for food, water, and shelter; social interaction; self-preservation; and reproduction.

Search for food, water, and shelter

Feeding behaviour (see pp.24–25) varies widely, and one of the main drives behind this is whether a species is predator or prey. Predators are creatures that hunt and eat other creatures. Owls (such as this tawny owl, right) and other birds of prey, lizards, foxes, and even spiders are predators within gardens. Their prey is the wildlife that is caught, killed, and eaten. Wild creatures need water to survive (see pp.34–35). They use shelter for warmth, to rest and make nests and homes, and as a place to find food and to feel safe from predators (see pp.36–37).

Social interaction

Wild species encounter each other in the garden as they do elsewhere, and it's possible to observe these interactions. These fox cubs (left) are play fighting to learn new skills. Some species are territorial; robins, for example, fiercely defend their territory from other robins. Different calls and behaviours may also be related to attracting a mate. There are worlds of wildlife that we will never experience such as the social interactions between insects at ground level due to their size.

BENEFICIAL SIDE-EFFECTS

Most activities of wild creatures are geared to their own survival, but some offer positive impacts as a side-effect. These behaviours have evolved to benefit both plants and wild creatures. For example, while gathering food such as nuts, squirrels and jays take them and bury them; if the nuts are forgotten they may germinate to grow the next generation. Birds eat berries and spread the seeds via their droppings. Pollinators gather nectar for themselves, pollinating flowers at the same time, so the plant can produce fruit or set seed.

Self-preservation

Prey animals move away if they feel threatened; they may also be camouflaged to avoid being spotted. Predators (such as this grass snake, left) often move fast to catch the food they need to survive. Hibernation is a strategy used by many species for surviving the winter cold.

Reproduction

Many species come to our gardens for shelter and a safe space to breed. Insects look for plants on which to lay eggs and crevices in which to breed, while amphibians (such as this frog, left) spend time in the water mating and laying spawn. Mammals may burrow in a bank or under a hedge to make homes in which to raise their young.

THE FOOD CHAIN

*A food chain is a way of explaining how
food (and energy) passes through
a group of species.*

The simplest way of looking at a food chain is in terms of the producer, the consumer (or prey), and the predator. The food chain described here is one that might occur in a garden, and includes both resident and visiting wildlife. A wildlife-friendly garden is a miniature ecosystem that provides something for all parts of the food chain; it is by supporting the whole chain that all the wildlife in a garden will thrive (see also pp.40–41). A food chain is made up of herbivores, which eat plant material, carnivores, which eat other living creatures, and omnivores, which eat a mix of plants and other wildlife. Many herbivores are at the lower end of the food chain, while carnivores are mostly higher up the chain. Detritivores feed on dead plant material and droppings, breaking it down and recycling essential nutrients in the garden.

Producers

Plants and plant materials are the basis of the food chain, using energy from the sun, along with carbon dioxide from the atmosphere and water, to make their own food. They emit oxygen as part of this process, providing the air many organisms need to breathe. Plants offer nutrition in many ways, from water to nectar, stems, leaves, berries, and seeds.

Primary consumers

The primary consumers are herbivores, feeding on plants. They are often insects, but can be mammals or birds that eat seeds or berries. These species will be food for larger predators such as other mammals and birds. In the soil are earthworms, woodlice, slugs, and snails; by eating and excreting the soil, they process it, and help plants to rot, adding nutrients to the system.

Top predators

These are creatures that do not have a predator but instead only eat species lower down the food chain. Examples include tawny owls and sparrowhawks (left) and other birds of prey, which eat consumers such such as garden birds and small mammals.

The food chain shows the energy flow through an ecosystem. The chain has four broad levels, but these are not fixed, and the reality is much more complex, forming an interconnected web of interactions.

RECYCLING NUTRIENTS

Another garden system, running alongside the food chain, is the nutrient cycle. In simple terms, as plants and animals die, they decay and are decomposed by invertebrates, bacteria, and other microorganisms, releasing the nutrients (such as nitrogen and carbon) back into the soil so they can be used again by plants as they grow. In a wildlife garden simple measures such as having a compost heap and allowing logs to rot down keeps more nutrients in the cycle.

Life

Secondary consumers

Small mammals, reptiles, amphibians, and birds typically eat the invertebrate primary consumers. Swifts eat flies, birds such as tits eat worms and caterpillars, and bats hunt moths. Invertebrates themselves have a hierarchy, because some prey on other invertebrates: for example, spiders eat flies, and some beetles eat smaller insects.

Decay

Death

THE GARDEN
AS REFUGE

THE GARDEN AS REFUGE

Our gardens are not only a refuge for us humans, they're a refuge for wildlife – or we can make them into one. No matter how small or large the space, we can encourage more wildlife to visit and perhaps stay. By focusing on what wildlife needs to survive – food, water, and shelter – and by planning to supply those needs, we can alter our gardens to work harder for wildlife. We can also stop using harmful chemicals, and adopt gardening techniques that support the complex garden ecosystem.

Dense ivy and fallen leaves make a warm, sheltered place for this bank vole to take cover.

A WILD AND AN UNWILD GARDEN

The differences between a garden that is wildlife friendly and one that isn't may not be as great as you expect.

Everyone wants something slightly different from their garden, from a place to sit with friends to a play space for children — that's what makes gardens individual and interesting. Whatever your aims for your garden, it's possible to make some simple adjustments to encourage more wildlife. The most important thing is to avoid using toxic chemicals, which indiscriminately destroy wildlife. The increasing use of plastic grass also offers nothing to wildlife. By avoiding these, and instead making small changes with wildlife in mind, you can bring your garden to life.

An unwild garden

Small elements in a garden can make it unfriendly to wildlife, even if the garden looks similar on the surface to one where lots of wildlife thrives. Barriers may physically discourage animals entering the garden. Using chemicals may deal with "pests" or weeds, but will deter or even actively harm the wildlife. A narrow range of plants may also limit the creatures that visit.

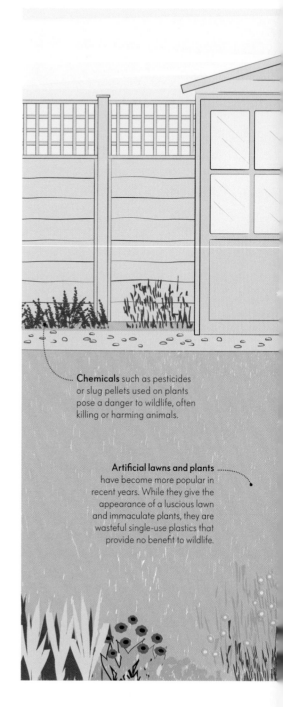

Chemicals such as pesticides or slug pellets used on plants pose a danger to wildlife, often killing or harming animals.

Artificial lawns and plants have become more popular in recent years. While they give the appearance of a luscious lawn and immaculate plants, they are wasteful single-use plastics that provide no benefit to wildlife.

A wild garden

A garden that's friendly to wildlife offers interest all year round in comparison to an unwild garden. A range of plants, and the use of real grass in the lawn, offers food sources and shelter for lots of species. Although a little more maintenance may be needed, the rewards make it worth it. Adding a water source and providing access into the garden will bring in more creatures. This helps to create a balance where some wildlife feeds on others, helping to reduce "pests" so that plants thrive.

An access hole in a fence allows hedgehogs to enter and exit a garden. Without these holes, fences and walls can form a barrier to wild creatures that don't have wings.

A water source is vital not only for birds, but for mammals, insects, and invertebrates to drink from, and even bathe in. Add a ramp for mammals to climb out, and for amphibians such as toads to bask upon.

Plant up your garden with wildlife in mind. In a smaller or mostly paved garden you can fill pots and hanging baskets. If you have open ground you can plant up borders. And make the most of vertical surfaces by planting climbers to grow up them. More plants encouraage insects, which then attract birds and even bats.

Toad

Sparrows

Wilder areas such as piles of fallen leaves, longer grass, and logs in damp places, help hedgehogs, toads, and frogs looking for somewhere to hibernate and shelter.

Orange-tip butterfly

Red admiral

NATURAL FOOD SOURCES

A successful garden ecosystem needs good foundations: soil, algae, decaying wood, and plants.

Every creature and plant in a garden can be considered a source of food, but our tidy gardens offer much less food for wildlife than wilder gardens. By exploring and being aware of the natural systems that have always supplied nutrition to wildlife, we can work with them to ensure that these food sources are abundant and provide food throughout the seasons. This means avoiding the use of harmful chemicals in the garden, leaving some plants to go to seed, and not being too tidy – at least in a few places. If necessary, we can also add extra feeders to top up natural food sources.

Soil

Soil contains nutrients, minerals, moisture, and gases that nourish and support all the plant life in the garden (see pp.60–61). Earthworms, beetles, and some small mammals will work through the soil looking for nutrients. Bacteria and fungi break down organic matter from plants, digesting them and releasing more nutrients.

Earthworms create tunnels in the soil, allowing in air to help the soil structure. Their worm casts are full of nutrients.

Dead wood

Fallen trees, logs, and autumn leaves are a vital source of food. Trees that have died and are left standing are also valuable. Springtails, woodlice, and other invertebrates use dead wood as a breeding ground, and break down the wood at the same time. Many creatures shelter under wood.

The great spotted woodpecker chips into soft wood on living trees and decaying wood on dead trees (left) looking for insects.

ADDITIONAL FOOD SOURCES

The best way to support garden wildlife is to provide natural food sources. However, gardens can rarely provide all the necessary nutrients, especially in winter when flowers and berries are scarce. Feeders for small mammals (pp.146–47) and birds (pp.118–19) can provide a much-needed boost.

Algae

Algae and phytoplankton are microscopic aquatic organisms that are the basis of diets for many water-dwelling creatures. Fish, crustaceans, worms, and tadpoles eat algae. Algae typically grow in water, although they can live in damp places such as pond edges where creatures such as birds, newts, and frogs can feast upon them. Too much algae can smother life in the pond, but a healthy balance helps wildlife.

Tadpoles are among the many water-dwelling creatures that feed on algae around the edge of a pond.

Flowers and plants

Every bit of a plant can be a source of food (see pp.60–61). Flowering plants are vital for pollinators, but trees and grasses as well as wild plants such as dandelions and nettles are all valuable to the wildlife of a garden.

Caterpillars usually feed on leaves, often becoming food for birds in turn.

NATURAL WATER SOURCES

Water is one of the key components for survival on Earth, as much for wildlife as it is for us.

Like humans, many wildlife species are made up of a high proportion of water, and they need to replenish it and keep hydrated day to day, as well as to keep clean. A natural environment provides a variety of water sources for wildlife to drink from – not just ponds or bird baths (see opposite). If you're aware of all these different sources, you can adjust what's in your garden, perhaps by introducing a broader range of plants, to ensure that moisture is easily accessible.

Gardening practices can also help to conserve water. If you keep your soil covered with plants, and add a layer of compost as a mulch, more water will remain in the soil for plants and invertebrates to access.

Dew and rain on leaves

Dew droplets in the morning and raindrops on rainy days offer tiny pools of hydration for small creatures to access. We can encourage these droplets to gather by ensuring we have shrubs and other plants in the garden with flat or bowl-shaped surfaces perfect for collecting water.

Flat leaves offer raindrops for insects to drink from the surface.

Pools and boggy ground

A damp or boggy area (see p.95) is a great way of introducing water naturally into the garden. These areas may occur in parts of the garden naturally, and offer a water source for insects, birds, and mammals as well as amphibians. Reptiles and amphibians also create pools in the ground to gather water. Most of the time they wiggle and wedge themselves into the ground to form a small crevice for water to collect. Boggy areas are an important aspect of a wildlife garden, so resist the temptation to drain or flatten them.

Insects can land on boggy gound and drink from water held by plants there.

ADDITIONAL WATER SOURCES

The two most popular ways to add water to a garden are by introducing a pond or a bird bath. Both are great sources of water, but it's essential to make sure that as many species as possible can access ponds safely (see p.95), and, in the case of a bird bath, to fill it up regularly to maintain a consistent supply. Some bird baths are tall and isolating for insects and small mammals, so choose carefully and adapt it to make it accessible if necessary (see pp.120–21).

Moisture from food

Wildlife doesn't just get hydration directly from water; a lot of moisture comes via natural food sources (see pp.116–17). Insects feed on sap from plants and they in turn provide moisture for birds, lizards, and others that feed upon them. Stems, leaves, fruits, and berries are also filled with water. Berries such as holly, hawthorn, and rowan offer valuable, accessible moisture when the ground and other water sources are frozen.

Berries are an important source of water as well as nutrients for birds such as this blackbird, butterflies, and small mammals.

SHELTER AND SAFETY

Safety is paramount for wildlife, and many species will only use gardens where they feel secure.

Providing shelter is a simple way to encourage wildlife into your garden. Wild creatures need shelter for a myriad of reasons. It allows them to feel safe from predators, and offers security for breeding, roosting, and even hibernating during winter months. They may also need a short break from fierce sun or a downpour of rain.

What makes good shelter?

Shelter must have adequate cover but still allow the wildlife to observe their surroundings. If the shelter is too close to windows and back doors there will be constant disturbance.

It helps to look at a garden in the same way that a wild creature might, assessing where the danger could be. This helps us to find a suitable place for introducing more natural shelter. For example, if there is only closely mown grass between a pond and the nearest vegetation, reptiles and amphibans may feel reluctant to run across the open space to cover; longer, unmown grass between would offer a safer way to move from one area to another.

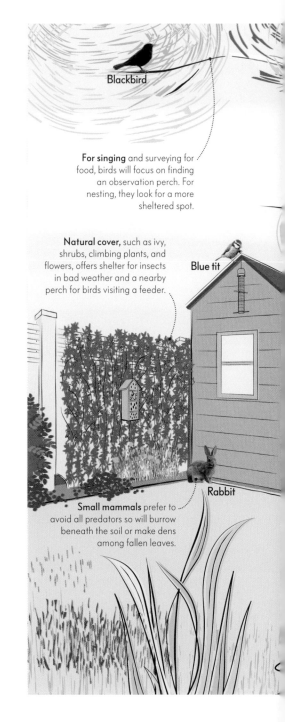

Blackbird

For singing and surveying for food, birds will focus on finding an observation perch. For nesting, they look for a more sheltered spot.

Natural cover, such as ivy, shrubs, climbing plants, and flowers, offers shelter for insects in bad weather and a nearby perch for birds visiting a feeder.

Blue tit

Small mammals prefer to avoid all predators so will burrow beneath the soil or make dens among fallen leaves.

Rabbit

ADDITIONAL SHELTER

To supplement natural shelter we can add all sorts of habitat boxes. There are bird boxes for nesting and roosting (see pp.124–25) as well as toad and frog houses (see p.99), bee and butterfly houses (see pp.66–69), and bat boxes (see pp.152–53). Shelter can also be as simple as a pile of logs or twigs behind a shrub, or a few unused plant pots tucked away behind the garden shed.

Evergreen shrubs offer shelter all year round; winter shelter is much harder to find for small creatures.

Insects will hide among the plants so they cannot be seen.

Wren

Common lizard

Drone fly

Reptiles choose an open place to bask, but with a space to rush to should a predator or risk emerge.

Aim for balance so that humans can have the open spaces they need to make the most of a garden, while there is always some form of cover nearby so that wildlife can also take shelter and move around.

PLANTING

*Whether you are planting a border from scratch, or
simply adding a few plants to an existing garden,
think about what each plant offers to wildlife.*

Choosing plants for a garden can be daunting, but if you keep the wildlife in mind, the task is much easier. Note the creatures that visit your own and neighbouring gardens, and the local area. Consider their needs. Does a local butterfly species need a certain caterpillar foodplant? Could a sparrow flock be tempted by a new tree?

Aim to include plants that flower at different times of year to offer a steady supply of pollen and nectar, as well as a mix of day- and night-opening flowers. Don't forget about winter, either: midwinter-flowering shrubs offer nectar to early-emerging bees, berries and seed heads can be a vital food source, while evergreens offer shelter when deciduous plants shed their leaves. Bear in mind the conditions in your garden. How big is it? How much sun does it get? Is the soil dry and free-draining? List some plants that you would like to introduce based on the conditions and your research. You don't want to plant something that will struggle in your space.

Arranging your plants

By thinking about your planting in layers (see right), you can design a border – or a whole garden – to appeal to wildlife. Grassy areas and low plants attract smaller creatures such as invertebrates and mice, and give shelter for birds and amphibians. In the mid-level, perennials and smaller shrubs offer flowers for pollinators, and predators will eat invertebrates that nibble the leaves and stems. Finally, climbers, large shrubs, or trees are safe spaces for birds to roost. Layering is good for humans, too: it draws our eye to the backdrop of the tallest plants, allowing us to enjoy the spectrum of greenery on display.

FRIEND OR FOE?

Love them or hate them, the plants that spring up uninvited, the wildflowers that many call "weeds", provide vital resources for wildlife. Dandelions are excellent plants for bees and other pollinators to feed upon. Nettles are another valuable wildlife plant. Caterpillars, particularly those of small tortoiseshell and peacock butterflies, use them as their food plants, while ladybirds and other insects feed on the aphids that use their leaves, and birds enjoy feeding on the caterpillars. Why not allow a few to grow in a corner of your garden or even to fill out your flower borders?

Trees

Trees provide the top layer of plants and offer shade, shelter, and food to insects, birds, and some mammals. Fruits, berries, and flowers are a vital part of the food chain, often at a time when other food is scarce. Leaves and bark crevices are a good source of water. In a smaller garden, you may not have space for your own tree, but if there is a neighbouring tree, it can form part of the layering ecosystem.

Shrubs and climbers

The upper-middle layer of plants is likely to be mainly shrubs and climbing plants. These are often dense and form great shelter for birds and other wildlife, including at ground level. Many offer flowers for pollinators and berries later in the year.

Plants for sunny areas

There is the greatest choice of plants for sunny spots, and these are most likely to be visited by pollinators. A variety of flowers through the year offers a steady supply of food.

Plants for shade

Shady areas can also offer flowers for pollinators but are vital for beetles and other invertebrates as well as some amphibians and small mammals.

Grass

Longer grass at the lawn edge offers shelter and food for insects and their predators. It also allows wildflowers to thrive, such as dandelions, clover, and buttercups.

GARDENING
FOR WILDLIFE

The key to wildlife-friendly gardening is
great soil health and an organic mindset.
Here are a few good practices to try.

Wildlife gardening isn't just about choosing the right plants, but following the right techniques and principles. These strengthen the ecosystem within your garden, and, once established, may also save you both money and time.

Making compost

Everyone with a little space to spare should make their own compost. Instead of having to buy heavy plastic bags from garden centres, you recycle kitchen and garden waste into nutritious, crumbly brown organic matter that will keep your garden in top condition. A compost heap can even be a habitat in its own right (see p.98).

Purpose-built compost bins can be bought cheaply (sometimes free from local councils), or built from wooden pallets. Material to add to the heap can be divided into "green" (grass cuttings, uncooked food waste, recently cut plant material) and "brown" (fallen leaves, shredded paper and card, straw). Aim for an equal split of brown and green, providing nitrogen from the green, and carbon from the brown. This balance ensures your heap doesn't have too much nitrogen, which

Worms and other detritivores rot down
the plant material in a compost heap.

will smell, or too much carbon, which slows the breakdown. Ensure no chemicals, including pesticides, are used on any waste entering the heap. It can take 6–12 months to produce compost, depending on the size of the bin and the amount of material.

NATURAL SLUG-REPELLENTS

Many of us love to grow fruit and vegetables in our gardens, but slugs and snails can cause issues by nibbling their way through crops. Many people reach for slug pellets and pesticides as a "solution", but these chemical-based repellents cause a huge amount of harm, not only to slugs and snails, but to the wider food chain (see pp.24–25). Hedgehogs, birds, and other small mammals that eat the dead slugs are often in turn killed by the poison.

That doesn't mean we have to accept slug-eaten crops. Natural solutions exist that either discourage these unwelcome visitors, or kill them without causing inadvertent harm to other garden wildlife:

- **A layer of eggshells** around your plants creates a sharp barrier that slugs and snails do not like to cross.
- **Used coffee grounds** are disliked by slugs and snails when spread around your planting areas.

Slugs appear to be repelled by caffeine, and larger amounts can even kill them. If you do not drink coffee, try your local coffee house.

- **Citrus fruits** are loved by molluscs. Add some halved citrus fruits into an area of your garden for slugs and snails to enjoy and to keep them away from your fruit and vegetables.
- **Seaweed** is rich in salt, which slugs and snails hate – making it a great repellent. Wash it to remove excess salt (it will still be salty enough), and spread it around your plants. As a bonus, it will give your soil an extra nutrient and mineral boost. Note: always check you have permission before gathering seaweed from the shore.

The best way to keep these so-called "pests" under control, however, is by creating a diverse ecosystem. Encourage song thrushes, hedgehogs, amphibians, and others to keep the slug population down.

No-dig gardening

"No-dig" is a fairly new way of gardening. It focuses on leaving the natural soil undisturbed, but layering materials and compost on top to create a new planting area, rather than stripping off the soil and digging it over. To convert an area of lawn into a no-dig bed, or improve existing bare soil, lay down sheets of cardboard and top with a thick layer of compost (see left), up to 20cm (8in) deep. Worms will pull down the compost, mixing it with the top layers of soil, and enriching it. The natural organisms and nutrients in the soil are preserved and can thrive. On an established bed, you add the compost each autumn as a mulch. By not disturbing the soil, you also avoid bringing weed seeds to the surface, so there will be less weeding to do.

A no-dig border made up of layers of cardboard and compost will be fertile and produce strong growth in the plants.

PLANNING A WILDLIFE GARDEN

Designing a wildlife garden is like designing any outdoor space. It's all about considering the wants and needs of those that'll use it.

Your garden needs to serve both humans and wildlife, maximizing the benefits for wildlife without making it unwelcoming or unusable for people. That's why planning is so important.

A good starting point is to make an overhead plan of what you already have. First, create a scale drawing of the garden as it is currently. Note down where it gets the most sun or shade, and at what times of day, as well as any particularly boggy or dry areas. Think about how you use it – both the fun stuff (eating dinner al fresco, playing football) and the necessities (where you keep the bins). Next, look at it from the point of view of different kinds of wildlife, noting down anything that your garden already does well.

Now, consider what changes you can make. This is just a plan, so you can be as ambitious as you like, and scale back some of the bigger ideas later if they are too much. Focus on the key elements: food, water, shelter, and access. Also think about what you can remove, such as paving, perhaps a wall that could become a hedge, and obstacles for wildlife. If children use your garden, you will also want to consider their needs as you make your plans (see pp.44–45).

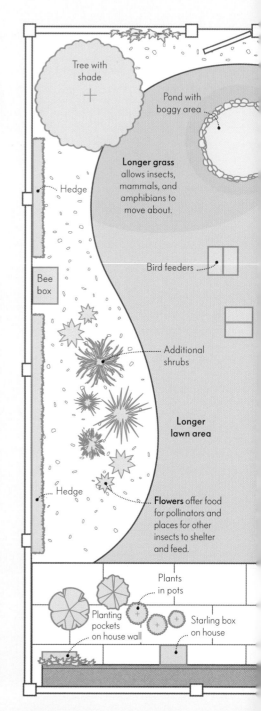

Tree with shade

Pond with boggy area

Longer grass allows insects, mammals, and amphibians to move about.

Hedge

Bird feeders

Bee box

Additional shrubs

Longer lawn area

Hedge

Flowers offer food for pollinators and places for other insects to shelter and feed.

Plants in pots

Planting pockets on house wall

Starling box on house

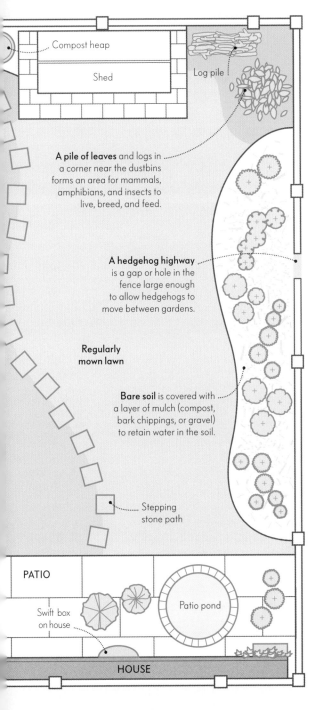

Compost heap

Shed

Log pile

A pile of leaves and logs in
a corner near the dustbins
forms an area for mammals,
amphibians, and insects to
live, breed, and feed.

A hedgehog highway
is a gap or hole in the
fence large enough
to allow hedgehogs to
move between gardens.

Regularly
mown lawn

Bare soil is covered with
a layer of mulch (compost,
bark chippings, or gravel)
to retain water in the soil.

Stepping
stone path

PATIO

Swift box
on house

Patio pond

HOUSE

Water sources

Small dishes of water, bird baths, and more
plants to hold water naturally are relatively easy
to add. On a larger scale, you could dig a pond,
or position a container pond on a paved area,
choosing a semi-shaded location that is not
under a tree. If you already have a pond, look at
how wildlife-friendly it is; access such as ramps,
shallow drinking areas, and pollinator-friendly
plants will all attract more wildlife (see pp.94–95).

Shelter

Consider adding shelter in the form of shrubs
and other plants near garden entrances such as
gates, gaps, and walls. Add roosting pockets and
nest boxes for birds and bats. Thorny shrubs and
strongly scented plants such as lavender deter
predators, while an area of longer grass provides
much-needed cover for creatures moving from
one area of your garden to another.

Access

If you have a fence, you can add small holes or
gaps at the base to form "hedgehog highways",
or allow a little gap under your gate. On a larger
scale, exchange walls for fences, hedges, and
shrubs. These attract more wildlife, and are
beautiful in their own right, adding colour
and variety at different times of year.

Food sources

Add a wide variety of flowering plants as natural
food sources that cater for insects, pollinators,
and birds. Left unmown, you may find that your
lawn will produce plenty of wildflowers – or you
could sow a wildflower seed mix in bare ground
to create a mini-meadow – even a small area of
wildflowers attracts a lot of insects. You can add
purpose-made feeders for birds (see pp.118–19)
and for small mammals (see pp.146–47).

**In this plan the existing features of the
garden are in white, with possible changes
and additions marked on in green. It helps
to look at the whole even if you're not going
to make all of the changes at once.**

A FAMILY-FRIENDLY WILDLIFE GARDEN

A wildlife garden bursting with life can't help but be appealing to children as well as adults, who can all share the space.

It's important to take your family's needs into account when planning to attract more wildlife to your garden. How children use the garden often changes as they grow older, so it's good to be flexible, too. Safety and space to play and explore are key considerations, and the garden needs to be robust enough for ball games and hide and seek. As more wildlife finds its way into your garden, children are likely to enjoy watching the interactions and identifying new visitors.

Consider adding your wildlife features in spaces where your children may not play, such as behind sheds or in the front garden. You can also include wildlife-friendly trees and plants at the edges. A wildlife garden is an opportunity to show children how animals behave, and how to respect rather than fear wildlife.

Avoiding possible dangers

When children are very young, they may not understand the potential dangers in a garden. Ponds can pose a risk for young children and may need to be adapted by putting a fence around the pond or a metal mesh over the top; or delay adding the pond until children reach an age when they are safe around deeper water. Situate compost bins and hibernaculums away from where young children can easily reach them; this will minimize disturbance of hibernating creatures, including snakes.

If you take an interest in the wild visitors to your garden, it's likely that your child may share that interest and become more aware of their surroundings.

Opportunities to learn

Arguably the greatest dangers posed by a wildlife garden are brought about by ignorance or misunderstandings. If we don't learn about wildlife behaviours, we're more likely to behave in a way that makes creatures feel threatened, which can in turn prompt them to react. That's true for all of us, but especially young children. But, to look at it another way, a wildlife garden can be a brilliant learning opportunity. Children soak up so much information, and educating them about wildlife, allowing them to have their

Involving children in looking after the garden helps them to learn in a safe environment about how plants grow, and what wildlife may make use of them.

space, keep their distance, and respect the creatures will allow both children and wildlife to thrive. Encourage them to participate in looking after the garden so they can see both the nettles that may sting and the amazing caterpillars that eat the nettles. You can share an enjoyment in wildlife by creating some of the projects in this book, such as pond dipping (see pp.102–103), and making a hibernaculum (see pp.100–101).

WILDING A SMALL SPACE

A small garden offers plenty of opportunities to encourage new and varied wildlife to visit.

It doesn't matter whether you have a courtyard garden or share your space with other residents, if your outdoor area is mainly paved over, or if all you have is a balcony. These are all places where wildlife can visit and even live.

In a smaller space you may not have ideal conditions for a full-scale wildlife garden, but you can add feeders and shelters to replicate more natural conditions. Birds in particular are adaptable and will take to a new environment without much hesitation, if there is adequate food and shelter for them to enjoy, and they feel safe. Likewise, insects and pollinators will enjoy whatever food and plants you choose to provide, especially in cities where natural food sources may be scarce. Depending on your situation, you can also expect to see mammals such as bats, and small mammals such as mice, voles, and hedgehogs if you offer suitable food and access.

Paved gardens

In a fully paved garden, containers are the answer for introducing plants. Choose containers that are light and easy to move, or upcycle some pallets and wood and create your own. Use peat-free compost for your plantings (see p.50). To ensure your containers work well for wildlife, group them to form a larger area of plants in layers so that wildlife can move and shelter among the pots. You can leave logs and fallen leaves as a hidden habitat behind pots.

This balcony is packed with plants on different levels and offers shelter and damp corners to hide as well as flowers.

Window feeders are perfect in small spaces and can allow you to get a close-up view of a bird as it's feeding.

Although space may be limited for natural food sources such as plants, you can focus on feeding stations. Bird feeders come in a range of sizes and types for different birds (see pp.118–19), so you can choose from these to offer a variety of food. There are feeding stations for hedgehogs and small mammals at ground level (see pp.146–47). Nest boxes for birds can be fixed to a wall (see pp.124–25). You can even create a mini-pond in an old sink or washing up bowl, adding some access points and pollinator-friendly plants.

Balconies

Flying insects and birds visit balconies, making regular stops if there is food or shelter for them. You can find bird feeders that attach to a window, or add some nectar-feeders which can be filled with sugar syrup and fruits, attracting bees and moths. Some bird boxes, such as those for swifts, can be put up high on a building or under house eaves.

Awkward spaces

Small spaces such as side alleys, garden steps, and even patios around garden structures, can all be adapted for wildlife. Windowboxes and container plants can be placed in corners. For vertical spaces, climbers or planting pockets filled with evergreen plants can look beautiful and provide pockets of shelter. Avoid being too tidy; fallen leaves offer food for invertebrates. Insect houses (see p.67) work in sun or shade. Ensure that anything placed or fixed high up or on steps is secured so it doesn't create a hazard.

A green wall is made up of a series of planting pockets with evergreen plants to make a mini vertical habitat.

SHARING
YOUR SPACE

*Sometimes our pets can cause issues with
the wildlife and birds in the garden, but there
are ways that we can help them to coexist.*

Cats and dogs are predators by nature. As pet owners, if we want a wildlife-friendly garden, we need to reduce the risk to wildlife without impacting on the pet's quality of life.

Cats

Killing tens of thousands of birds and small mammals each year, cats are major garden predators. Although we cannot guarantee they will never attempt to attack birds and small

mammals, there are measures that we can take to reduce the damage they do.

- **A bell on a collar** of a cat will make a sound as the cat moves, warning birds or mammals that the cat is present and may be about to attack. Ensure the collar fits snugly, but that it has a quick release should the cat get tangled in a hedge or twiggy undergrowth.

- **Feeding** your cat at around the same time as you fill your feeders ensures that the cat is well-fed before it goes outside so it may be less likely to go hunting.

- **Keep your cat in** for an hour before sunset and an hour after sunrise. This gives birds in the garden a chance to feed and roost, or wake up and feed. Alternatively, keep it in overnight so that it is unable to hunt for small mammals and bats.

- **Neutering** or spaying a cat typically makes it stay closer to home, which gives you more control over the area you can protect.

Although a cat with a collar may still stalk a bird or mouse, its prey may hear the bell and have time to flee.

Dogs need space to exercise and play.
Consider a dedicated fenced dog area so
other parts of the garden are undisturbed.

- **Protect bird feeders** by building up the surrounding plants with thornier varieties including roses at the base to offer a physical barrier. Plant bushes of lavender and lemon thyme nearby as cats may be deterred by the strong scents.
- **Discourage unwanted cats** by spreading citrus halves and peel around your bird feeders. Proprietary cat deterrents are also available to buy.

Dogs

Although dogs are less dangerous to wildlife than cats, they can nonetheless cause a nuisance by digging up the garden or by chasing and scaring birds, squirrels, reptiles, and other ground mammals, and even disturbing nests. Forcing wild species to flee can be more damaging in winter when food (and energy) is in short supply.

Consider leaving dogs a space of their own where they can play and dig to their heart's content. Hedging by itself may not keep the dog in the garden; instead, plant shrubs or climbers beside fencing to provide cover for wildlife while also keeping your dog secure. Lock your dog in at night to avoid encounters with nocturnal creatures such as hedgehogs.

BEYOND THE GARDEN

As well as making our gardens more wildlife-friendly, we must think about the wider environment, too. By making careful choices and working together, we can improve the conditions for wild creatures beyond the garden.

In the wider world, wildlife is faced with habitats that are fragmented and reducing in size due to pressures from housing, roads, farming, and industry. Many previously common species are in decline. Gardens can play a vital role in offering a safe haven for wildlife to eat and shelter. They can also form a bridge to link verges, parks, and other wild areas so that creatures can move freely from place to place.

Having wildlife in our gardens is all about sharing our spaces and supporting a variety of species. Although our gardens can be an oasis for wildlife, they work even better alongside other gardens. Try encouraging neighbours to adopt wildlife-friendly practices, using your own garden as a positive example. You could cooperate to create pollinator corridors where insects can fly between gardens, feeding on pollen-rich plants, and hedgehog highways through which wildlife can move around from garden to garden.

Plastic pollution

Plastic causes havoc in the environment, and can be a danger to wildlife. Avoid making the problem worse by using alternatives to plastic in your garden. If you throw away or even recycle plastic, you are passing the problem along, possibly to where it can harm wildlife elsewhere. If you have plastic plant pots, wash and reuse them year after year.

The problem with peat

One key environmental issue faced by gardeners is the presence of peat in commercially sold compost. Peat is harvested from natural bogs and wetlands, where it has taken thousands of years to accumulate. These bogs are fantastic and unique habitats supporting a huge range of plants and wildlife. Peat is carbon-rich and soaks up moisture like a sponge, which is why it is such a popular growing medium – but harvesting it causes that carbon to be released, contributing to climate change, and the drying out of peatlands, destroying the habitat. With this in mind, use only peat-free composts in the garden (or make your own, see p.40). Additionally, many nursery plants are grown and sold in peat-based composts, so wherever possible raise your own plants from seed or cuttings, or look for ones grown in peat-free compost.

Clockwise from top: an insect hotel offers shelter for many species; a fence allowing access between gardens enables hedgehogs and other small mammals to travel further; compostable cardboard seedling pots are a great alternative to plastic; a "dead hedge" of branches that have been cut down provides food and shelter in a park between gardens.

INSECTS
AND OTHER
INVERTEBRATES

INSECTS AND OTHER INVERTEBRATES

Invertebrates are an incredibly important group of species, often overlooked. They include insects, ranging from pollinators such as bees, butterflies, and beetles, to the less glamorous creatures like worms, slugs, and snails. Together, the species covered in this chapter are the basis of a thriving wildlife garden. This chapter looks at what invertebrates need to flourish, and how to provide for these needs – in order to support the ecosystem of the garden as a whole.

The violet ground beetle lives in leaf litter and under logs, and comes out to hunt slugs, snails, and insect larvae.

POLLINATING INSECTS

A pollinator is a creature that transfers pollen from one plant to another. Insects are the main pollinators of many plant species.

Bees, butterflies, moths, and beetles are all insect pollinators. They visit flowers to feed on nectar, and some gather pollen as a protein source. These insects transfer pollen from plant to plant as they visit flowers – often accidentally as it collects on hairs on their bodies and rubs off on other flowers. Pollinators are active at different times: bees and butterflies tend to be diurnal feeders, active during the day, while most moths are nocturnal feeders. As some flowers close in the dark, night-flying pollinators visit different blooms than day-flying ones, including honeysuckle and evening primrose.

What plants do pollinators need?

The greater the variety of flowering plants on offer, the more pollinators will visit. Pollinators need a range of plants that flower over a long period of time so they have a consistent food source. Spring is when many pollinators emerge; some, such as queen bumblebees, forage for nectar and pollen from early-flowering plants to give them energy to start up a new colony. Late spring and summer sees the widest selection of plants and is the peak for many pollinators who need energy to lay eggs and feed colonies. Toward the autumn, later-flowering plants such

LIFECYCLE OF AN INSECT

Insects have a number of stages in their lifecycle. For many insects, including butterflies, moths, bees, ants, and beetles, eggs are laid, and these hatch to produce larvae (or caterpillars in the case of moths and butterflies). These feed and grow until they form a pupa (or chrysalis), from which the adult insect, usually looking completely different from the larva, emerges.

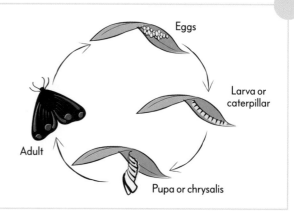

Eggs

Larva or caterpillar

Pupa or chrysalis

Adult

as ivy and Michaelmas daisies provide nectar for those pollinators that are still around on warmer days late in the year. It's not just about bedding plants and wildflowers, either. Blossom on trees such as apple, blackthorn, and horse chestnut provides a huge amount of nectar, and the pollinators in turn allow trees to set fruit.

The shape of a flower often determines which insects can access the nectar and pollen. In turn, the shape of the pollinators' mouthparts, including the long, sucking proboscis, is only suitable for certain flowers; they have evolved together. Flowers with a simple, "buttercup"-type shape are easiest for most insects to access. Others have flat heads of multiple flowers, while some are bell-shaped. Native and non-native flowers can be equally valuable for pollinators.

When selecting plants to support pollinators, consider all stages in the insect's lifecycle. Butterflies and moths need wide leaves, usually of specific food plants, to lay their eggs upon. Larvae feed on different food sources; caterpillars of the peacock butterfly feed on nettles, for example. They choose to attach the pupae to strong, sturdy, well-camouflaged stems or leaves before emerging as adults.

Wind-pollinated plants

Some flowers are wind-pollinated so have no need of insects to porduce seeds. These tend to be conifers, trees with catkins, such as hazel or willow, cereals and other crops, and grasses. All have inconspicuous flowers, and don't produce nectar. However, a few of these, including willow, are a great source of early pollen for bees, even if the bees do not play a role in pollination.

FLOWER SHAPES

Flat flower head
A flat flower head, such as dandelion (above), sunflower, or apple blossom is easy for pollinators to access.

Tubular flowers
Foxgloves (above) have a large circular opening into a tube that pollinators crawl into. Lavender and buddleia are also tubular, but pollinators access these with their tongue.

Double flowers
Many garden plants, such as some roses (above) and dahlias, are bred to have double flowers filled with petals. These may not contain nectar, and if they do, pollinators can't access it.

Among the flowers

Predatory ladybirds and bush-crickets eat aphids on flowers and plants. Spiders create webs among pollen-rich flowers where they wait for flies to become entangled.

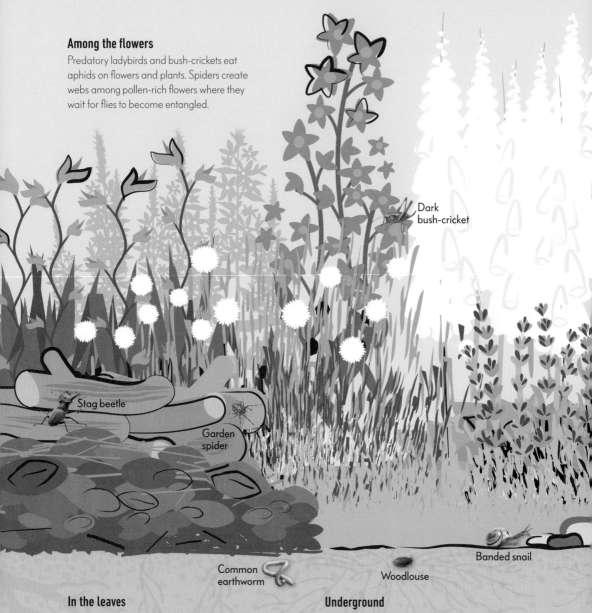

Dark bush-cricket

Stag beetle

Garden spider

Common earthworm

Woodlouse

Banded snail

In the leaves

Invertebrates thrive in leaf litter and log piles. Typically hunters such as some beetles lurk among the leaves waiting for their prey (often smaller invertebrates) to walk past. Slugs and snails also forage under leaf litter. Removing fallen leaves takes away a prime hunting habitat for these invertebrates; this is why a tidy garden is less attractive to wildlife.

Underground

Decomposers and detritivores are found within the soil, where they break down decaying matter under and on the surface. Worms consume and break down rotting plant matter, which is then excreted and added into the soil, providing nutrients. Woodlice, springtails, and beetles are also part of the range of decomposers, eating wood and decaying plants.

INVERTEBRATES IN THE GARDEN

Not all insects and invertebrates are pollinators – but all have a vital role to play in the garden ecosystem.

Non-pollinating invertebrates such as woodlice, slugs, snails, and worms all thrive in gardens. They are the primary consumers in the food chain (see pp.24–25), found all over the garden, feeding mostly on plant material, recycling nutrients, and foraging for food.

Blue-tailed damselfly

Ladybird

Around water

Insects and invertebrates are commonly found in and around garden ponds and pools, no matter the size. Adult dragonflies, damselfies, mayflies, and stoneflies thrive above water; they lay their eggs into the water and hunt smaller insects above the surface. For more about invertebrates in the water, see pp.108–109.

Water hoglouse

HEALTHY PLANTS, HEALTHY INVERTEBRATES

Living or decaying, plants are a key food source for insects and other invertebrates. The variety and health of plants will have an impact on the whole garden ecosystem.

To have healthy plants as food sources for insects and invertebrates, we first need to have good soil health. Soils can be acidic, alkaline, or neutral. These qualities are local, depending on the rocks that underlie the soil, and affect the plants that will grow there. Whatever the soil type, it will be improved in texture and nutrient levels by adding some home-made compost (see p.40). Spread a thick layer of compost as a mulch on to the soil between plants in your garden, preferably in early spring and late autumn, and invertebrates such as worms will carry the compost down, mixing it with the soil and releasing nutrients.

AVOIDING WEEDKILLERS

We often consider plants that make their way into our gardens naturally as "weeds". However, many, such as nettles and dandelions, are key foodplants and nectar sources for pollinators, and should be embraced in a wilder garden. If you decide you want to remove these plants, avoid weedkillers at all costs; they not only affect plants near the "weed" you are aiming to remove, but also harm micro-organisms in the soil, disrupting feeding patterns and changing their biology. Here are some chemical-free ideas:

- Remove them by hand with a hoe, hand fork, or trowel.
- Prevent light reaching weed seeds in the soil by mulching (see above) or adding more plants to beds and borders.
- Use no-dig gardening methods (see p.41) to avoid bringing fresh weed seeds to the surface.

Slugs, snails, and other invertebrates such as caterpillars eat the leaves.

Microscopic filaments of fungi grow through the soil connecting roots of plants to other roots and enabling them to absorb nutrients.

Earthworms make tunnels under the soil, providing oxygen to the roots of plants.

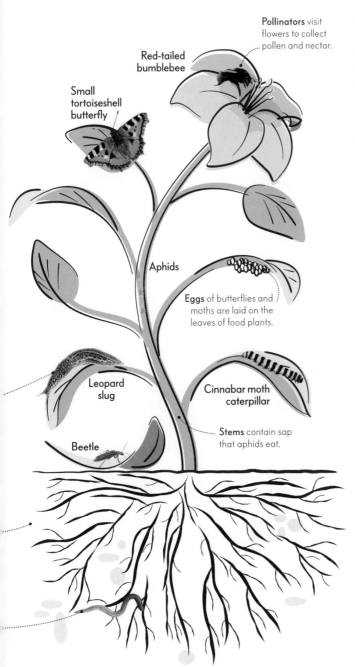

Pollinators visit flowers to collect pollen and nectar.

Red-tailed bumblebee

Small tortoiseshell butterfly

Aphids

Eggs of butterflies and moths are laid on the leaves of food plants.

Leopard slug

Cinnabar moth caterpillar

Stems contain sap that aphids eat.

Beetle

Nectar and pollen

To attract pollinators, it's vital to add pollen- and nectar-rich flowers to a garden. Sunflowers, hellebores, cornflowers, and buddleia are all full of nectar and pollen. Aim for a year-round supply in your garden by planting spring, summer, autumn, and winter-flowering plants. Fallen fruit from trees and brambles will provide sugars similar to nectar during autumn and winter months.

Leaves and stems

Aphids feed on plant stems, while ants "farm" the aphids, protecting them so they can feed on the honeydew they prduce. Other invertebrates such as ladybirds and their larvae feed on aphids, helping to keep a balance in the ecosystem. Butterflies and moths lay their eggs on plants that their caterpillars will like to eat once they hatch. In a wildlife garden, it's important to provide food for larvae and caterpillars, as well as adults, to encourage a richer variety of insects.

Roots

Decaying roots are food for invertebrates, which recycle the nutrients back into the soil. The process works both ways as worms, beetles, ants, and other invertebrates loosen and tunnel into the soil, making it a better environment for roots to grow, with more access to oxygen.

WATER SOURCES FOR INSECTS

Insects and invertebrates stay hydrated in the garden through a variety of means. Providing extra water helps them when natural sources dry up in warm weather.

Sap

The sap that flows through trees and plant stems, moving water and nutrients around the plant, also provides moisture to insects and invertebrates. Ants and beetles have chewing mouthparts that allow them to nibble into tree bark for sap, whereas aphids and other insects rely on sucking mouthparts to consume sap.

Plant surfaces

Plants provide hydration through the moisture on their leaves, stems, berries, and flower heads. Rainwater and dew also gathers in crevices and among roots. In prolonged dry weather, water your plants regularly – not only to keep the plants themselves healthy, but also to provide moisture for insects and invertebrates.

MAKE YOUR OWN SUGAR SYRUP

Bumblebees hibernate in the winter, but occasionally queens are late to go into hibernation, and may emerge early to start their new spring colony – and may struggle to find enough flowers with nectar to support them. As well as planting early-flowering varieties (see pp.184–85), you can help with simple sugar syrup. Dissolve 2–3 tablespoons of sugar in the same amount of hot water, and leave to cool. Place a drop near the bee. Alternatively, pour it into a shallow dish, add a few pebbles that sit above the syrup line, and place in the garden for queen bumblebees to perch on for a drink. Replenish regularly while it is needed.

Saucers and dishes

Among your flower beds or even within a plant pot, place a small saucer of water filled with stones or pebbles to allow garden pollinators and other insects to stand on a stone and have a drink without falling in. Ensure the water is not more than halfway up the stones so that the insects and invertebrates will not get stuck and the pollen on bees' legs will not get damp.

Ponds and damp areas

A shallow, sloping edge to a pond, or plants with floating leaves such as frogbit, will offer a safe place where insects can stand and drink from the water. Boggy areas of the garden also enable creatures to easily access water without the likelihood of drowning.

NATURAL SHELTER AND HABITATS

Plants and other garden features are vital for many insects to nest in, burrow in, hibernate, lay their eggs, and shelter their pupae.

Insects need shelter at all stages in their lifecycle, from the protection of a leaf when they emerge from their egg to a nook in which to hide from heavy rain, evade predators, or breed. A wild garden should provide all kinds of shelter – and while it is possible to create a dedicated space (see pp.66–67), the best place to start is simply by offering a range of habitats where visitors can make themselves at home.

Mixed planting

Having areas of dense, bare, tall, and short vegetation allows a variety of insects and invertebrates to thrive. Butterflies lay their eggs on caterpillar foodplants. Earwigs use stems as an entrance point into the soil, and spiders create their webs between plants to catch flying insects.

Ground level

Ants make their nests in the soil, and beetles also lay their eggs there. Worms make their homes in burrows underground, while slugs spend the day just under the surface. Then there's a type of insect you might not expect to find at ground level: bees. White-tailed bumblebees and common carder bees nest under tufts of grass, while abandoned rodent holes are ideal for bumblebees to establish a colony. Providing longer areas of grass in your garden will give enough shelter for these bee species and other ground nesters to create nesting locations.

Trees

Earwigs, woodlice, centipedes, and millipedes all live and breed within trees, mainly in crevices and gaps in the bark. As their name suggests, tree bumblebees prefer to nest in holes in tree bark – although they may also use house eaves, compost heaps, and bird boxes.

Decaying wood

Fallen logs and other dead wood provides a great habitat and shelter for invertebrates such as spiders, beetles, and woodlice. Worms, slugs, and snails all use this habitat for feeding and surviving away from predators such as reptiles and birds. It's also a breeding ground for small invertebrates such as millipedes.

Walls and hard surfaces

Walls can provide a home for ladybirds and spiders. Many spiders use the mortar to create their tunnels, then prey on insects that pass by. Masonry bees and mining bees nest in individual holes that they make in banks, mortar joints, soft bricks, and within ivy on walls of older buildings. These do not create serious damage to buildings, as the bees simply enlarge existing holes. Although each hole has one occupant, the holes are often grouped together with several bees nearby.

HUMAN-MADE SHELTER

It's possible to make or buy additional shelter for insects. You can tailor each structure to meet the needs of a particular species.

If you can't provide a wide range of natural habitats for insects and invertebrates (see pp.64–65) – or if you want to offer an extra helping hand – purpose-built shelters are a great solution. Many of these shelters can be mounted on a wall, shed, or fence where the insects can fly or crawl in and out in relative safety, and where it may also be possible to observe them. The sight of a leafcutter bee slowly covering the entrance hole after laying an egg is mesmerizing.

Dome for social bees

Arguably the simplest bee habitat you can create is a dome for social bees – such as bumblebees –which live in a colony with a queen. This provides a place for breeding and overwintering. You need a ceramic plant pot with a hole in the base. Place it, upside down, over a small mound of soft soil, sinking the rim well into the soil (but keeping the hole above ground). For how to make a wooden bumblebee hotel, see pp.68–69.

Solitary bee hotel

Solitary bees find or make holes to lay eggs in. Some such as mason and leafcutter bees, which nest in hollow stems, may use a solitary bee hotel. Placed on the ground or fixed to a sunny post with a nail or screw, this "hotel" is a box containing a series of long tubes, such as bamboo or old plant stems. The female solitary bee enters at one end, lays an egg, provided with pollen and nectar, before sealing the hole. The young bee hatches, eats the pollen and nectar, and exits the hole.

Ladybird tower

Ladybirds and other invertebrates such as earwigs, woodlice, and centipedes crawl inside this wooden structure via a small hole to a larger central space, filled with straw, where they roost in the evening and hibernate in winter. Fix it to a fence, shed, or tree.

Roof keeps the structure mostly dry and sheltered.

Straw offers places for ladybirds and other beetles.

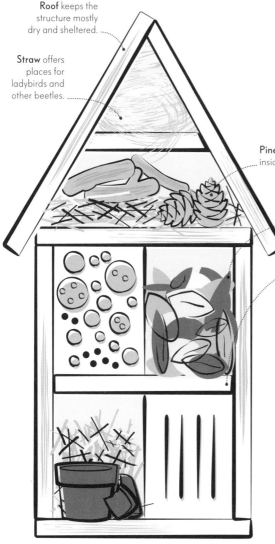

Pine cones are warm and dry inside for ladybirds to hibernate.

Dead wood and loose bark attracts spiders, woodlice, centipedes, and beetles.

Shelves separate different areas so a variety of nests can be added.

Insect house

Insect houses come in a range of shapes and sizes to buy, and are relatively easy to make, too. They provide a sheltering and roosting space for butterflies, moths, and other insects, especially in winter. Within the structure there can be mini-habitats such as holes for bees, and leaves and broken plant pots for small invertebrates. For butterflies, vertical slots cut into wood mimic the crevices in tree bark in which butterflies shelter from bad weather or predators. You can install insect houses in different locations for different species, such as in sunlight for bees or in shade for woodlice, earwigs, moths, and beetles.

MAKE YOUR OWN BUMBLEBEE HOTEL

It's relatively quick, easy, and inexpensive to make your own bee hotel, providing nesting space in a sunny, sheltered spot.

Bumblebees are social bees that live in colonies. In summer they may raise larvae in the box, and in winter they may hibernate there. The location determines which bees use it: a tree for tree bumblebees, on the ground for common carder bees (a type of bumblebee), or in vegetation for buff-tailed bumblebees. The box has a nesting chamber, which can be filled with soft material. An entrance chamber protects the nest from birds and small mammals in search of the larvae and eggs. Little maintenance is needed, but when there is less activity, in spring and autumn, you can check the wood is sound and prise off or unscrew the top to replenish the nesting material.

YOU WILL NEED

- Untreated wood from a sustainable source (1cm/½in thick)
- Tape measure and pencil
- Hand saw
- Hole saw
- Hammer or drill
- Nails or screws (50mm/2in)
- Nesting material (hay, moss, sawdust, or grass cuttings)

1. Mark out and cut the box pieces

Using a tape measure and pencil, measure and mark out on your pieces of wood all the sections of the box you will need, as shown below. Check all the measurements again, then cut the pieces.

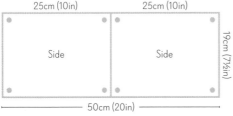

25cm (10in)   25cm (10in)

Side   Side

19cm (7½in)

50cm (20in)

17cm (6¾in)   17cm (6¾in)   17cm (6¾in)   25cm (10in)   25cm (10in)

Front   Barrier   Back   Top   Bottom

Access hole

Nail hole

17cm (6¾in)

101cm (40in)

2. Make the access holes

Using a hole saw, cut a 2.5cm (1in) hole in the centre of the front, and two in the barrier. These will provide the bees with access to the chamber; the barrier will keep predators out.

3. Nail together the box

Fix the front, back, top, and bottom together with nails. Create the nesting chamber by nailing the barrier piece about one-quarter of the way along the box from the front.

4. Finish and position the box

Nail on one of the sides, then add nesting material to the chamber. Nail on the final side. Place the completed box in your desired location. This box (right) has been positioned slightly raised and among lavender to attract buff- and white-tailed bumblebees.

OBSERVING INVERTEBRATES

To find out which invertebrates share your garden, it's a good idea to observe them systematically a couple of times a year.

If you've ever lifted a stone or moved a plant pot, you'll have encountered some of the insects and invertebrates that have made a home in your garden. Earthworms, woodlice, springtails, slugs, snails, and the odd beetle – these and more will lurk in dark, damp, undisturbed spots. Grasses, flowers, and wood piles are all inhabited by garden invertebrates such as ants, beetles, and grasshoppers. Locating invertebrates is a great activity for involving children, too. Spring and summer are when you will spot most insects and invertebrates but it's possible to find them all year.

By identifying and recording the invertebrate species you find in your garden, you can build up a picture of what creatures are active at different times of year. It can also help you to monitor whether numbers are increasing as you make your garden more wildlife-friendly. Not every creature needs to be collected. Some species that are hunting, such as wolf spiders in their holes, can be identified through their behaviour and by sight rather than disrupting their habitats.

1. Locate and collect

Identify a few key habitats in your garden (see pp.58–59) and observe which invertebrates come and go. To collect an invertebrate, gently sweep it with a soft paintbrush into a clear pot. Do not use your hands, as this can transfer oils and toxins onto the body. Collect one species at a time.

2. Identify

Take a close look at the invertebrates you have collected. Turn to pages 72–83, which feature a selection of common and interesting species. Alternatively, look at a more specialist reference book or app. If you can't find the creature straightaway, take a picture to help identify it later.

3. Record and release

Record the species you've found, taking notes or pictures. Release the invertebrates gently where you found them; avoid keeping them for more than about 5 minutes. Consider uploading your findings to an app, or sharing them with a local wildlife group or online (see pp.82–83).

HUNTING FOR MOTHS

Set up a moth trap

A moth trap uses a bright light to attract night-flying moths to an entrance to an area lined inside with old egg boxes or similar materials. Moths fly in and are trapped until the following day. Place the trap where it won't catch the morning sun and heat up too much.

Inspect the moths that are caught

The next day the moths are often still and so are easier to identify before letting them go into dense vegetation. This is a swallow-tailed moth (above).

Yellow
shoulder band

Fluffy ginger ....
upper body

BUFF-TAILED BUMBLEBEE
Bombus terrestris

Size Worker (female) and male: 11–17mm (½–⅝in); queen: 20mm (¾in) long.

ID features Black across upper body and abdomen, yellow bands across shoulders and abdomen. Queen has an off-white tail; worker and male have a whiter tail.

Habitat Varied, including lowland, rural, and urban areas.

Feeding Nectar-rich plants, including white clover, comfrey, lavender, and forget-me-not.

Breeding Nests underground; will use a bumblebee box. Queen is often seen March to August, sometimes from January. Workers hatch in early summer; males later in summer.

RED-TAILED BUMBLEBEE
Bombus lapidarius

Size Worker (female): 11–17mm (½–⅝in); male: 14–16mm (⅝in); queen: 20mm (¾in) long.

ID features Queen and worker easily recognizable with black body and bright red tail; male has a yellow face and shoulder band.

Habitat Chalk grassland, woods, heathland, gardens.

Feeding Nectar-rich plants, including bluebell, crocus, blackthorn, vetch, bird's-foot trefoil; also visits dead-nettle, ivy, and gorse.

Breeding Nests under stones or in burrows in clay banks. Queen emerges from hibernation in spring, seen April to October; workers from April; males and new females later in summer.

Worker
(female)

COMMON CARDER BEE
Bombus pascuorum

Size Worker (female): 10mm (½in); male: 12–14mm (½in); queen: 13mm (½in) long.

ID features Very fluffy, with a ginger patch on upper body. Worker, male, and queen very similar in appearance, but queen is larger.

Habitat Farmland, gardens, woodlands, and hedgerows.

Feeding Visits tubular flowers such as heather, clover, lavender, and foxglove; also sweet peas.

Breeding Nests in cavities and mossy lawns; will use a bumblebee box. Queen emerges from hibernation in early spring and can be seen March to October. Worker bees fly in early summer; males slightly later.

TREE BUMBLEBEE
Bombus hypnorum

Size Worker (female): 10–16mm (½–⅝in); male: 13mm (½in); queen: 15mm (⅝in) long.

ID features Distinct ginger patch on the upper body and black elsewhere. Tail is white, with females having a larger patch of white than males. Queens similar to worker and male bees although larger.

Habitat Woodlands, and gardens with wooded areas.

Feeding Visits flowers of soft fruit such as raspberry and blackberry, also fuchsia and lime tree.

Breeding Nests in tree cavities and buildings; will use bumblebee nesting boxes or old bird boxes. Queen emerges from hibernation in early spring and can be seen February to July. Workers hatch in spring; males follow in May and June.

Female

LEAF-CUTTER BEE
Megachile spp.

Size Female and male: 5–12mm (¼–½in).

ID features Dark body; underside of abdomen has orange hairs in female. Solitary bee, identifiable from its behaviour of cutting leaves.

Habitat Widespread, including gardens.

Feeding Visits flowers that are a rich source of pollen, such as catmint, heather, buddleia, and sunflower.

Breeding Nests in plant stems, dead wood, holes in cliffs, and old walls. Also uses bee hotels. Female cuts discs out of leaves and sticks them together with saliva to make a nest where their larvae will live. Can be seen late May to September. Larvae remain in chrysalis throughout winter and emerge the following year.

RED MASON BEE
Osmia bicornis

Size Female and male: 5–10mm (¼–½in) long.

ID features Black head with buff upper body; distinctive, ginger, fluffy abdomen. Slender body. Solitary bee.

Habitat Primarily in urban environments.

Feeding Visits cranesbill, borage, lavender, dandelion, and fruit tree blossom.

Breeding Nests in cavities within old buildings, mortar, and bricks; will also nest in dead wood and bare soil. Female digs and creates hole in which to lay eggs; holes are often grouped together. Also nests in bee hotels. Adults emerge in spring, the males a little before the females, and can be seen March to June. New adults from the season remain in their cocoons in a state of torpor over winter.

Long mouthpart for drinking nectar

BEE-FLY
Bombyliidae

Size Around 10mm (½in) long.

ID features Family of flies, of which 2 visit gardens. One has dark front edges across the upper body, the other has speckles. Distinguishable from bees and wasps by its long proboscis (mouthpart); has 2 wings rather than 4.

Habitat Varied, including gardens, woodlands, cliffs.

Feeding Visits a wide range of flowers, including daisy, forget-me-not, sweet pea, violet, and primrose. Larvae are parasites of solitary bees and wasps.

Breeding Emerges in early spring and can often be seen March to June.

DRONE FLY
Eristalis tenax

Size 10–12mm (½in) long.

ID features A hoverfly with brown and orange markings on a dark body. Looks similar to a honey bee, but with 2 wings rather than 4.

Habitat Gardens, farmland, heathland, woodland, wetlands, urban areas; larvae found in muddy water.

Feeding Adult feeds on nectar and is efficient pollinator; visits a range of plants, including ivy, before it hibernates. Larvae feed on decaying matter in water.

Breeding Adult hibernates from October to February, in milder climates from November to January. Larvae (also known as rat-tailed maggots) develop underwater.

Brown and orange markings

Leaf-like veins
on wing

Male

BRIMSTONE
Gonepteryx rhamni

Size Caterpillar: up to 35mm (1⅜in); adult wingspan:
60–74mm (2⅜–3in).

ID features Adult male is bright yellow, female very
pale green. Leaf-like wing shape. Bright green caterpillar.

Habitat Mainly scrub grasslands and woodlands,
but found in many habitats.

Feeding Caterpillar feeds on buckthorn and alder
buckthorn leaves; adult on nectar-rich plants, such
as thistle and bluebell.

Breeding Adults come out of hibernation then lay
eggs in early spring. New adults emerge in summer
to feed until hibernation in autumn.

PEACOCK
Aglais io

Size Caterpillar: up to 44mm (1¾in); adult wingspan:
63–68mm (2½–2⅝in).

ID features Butterfly has striking "eye spots" on upper
wings, underside almost black. Caterpillar is black with
white spots and short spines.

Habitat Widespread in both lowland and upland
areas; often visits gardens.

Feeding Caterpillars feed on leaves of
stinging nettles; adults on nectar-rich plants,
such as dandelion, buddleia, and teasel.

Breeding Adults come out of
hibernation then lay eggs in
spring on nettle leaves. New
adults emerge in July and August
before going into hibernation.

SPECKLED WOOD
Pararge aegeria

Size Caterpillar: up to
28mm (1in); adult wingspan:
46–56mm (1¾–2¼in).

ID features Butterfly is chocolate
brown with paler patches from cream to
pale orange. Bright green caterpillar with dark green
stripe down the back.

Habitat Mainly in woodland but anywhere with
shaded areas, including hedgerows and gardens.

Feeding Caterpillar feeds on grasses such as brome,
cock's foot, and common couch; adult on aphid
honeydew, and bramble flowers when aphids are scarce.

Breeding Adults emerge in spring, with a second
generation in summer and sometimes a third in
autumn. Uniquely, can overwinter as a larva or pupa in
plant material.

HOLLY BLUE
Celastrina argiolus

Size Caterpillar: up to 12mm (½in); adult wingspan:
26–33mm (1–1⅜in).

ID features Bright blue butterfly; female has black
wing edges whereas male has blue to the edge.
Caterpillar is light green with white and pinkish-brown
spots and streaks.

Habitat Gardens, churchyards, woodland.

Feeding Caterpillars feed on buds, flowers, and berries
of holly and ivy; adults on tree sap, aphid honeydew,
nectar, and the juices from rotting fruit and flesh.

Breeding Adults are seen from March onwards.
A second and sometimes third brood emerges in
summer. They may overwinter in chrysalis form.

Blue dots at wing edge ....

SMALL TORTOISESHELL
Aglais urticae

Size Caterpillar: up to 30mm (1¼in); adult wingspan: 50–55mm (2–2⅛in).

ID features Butterfly is red-orange with black and yellow patches on the fore wings, and blue spots around the wing edge. Black caterpillar with yellow-white spines.

Habitat Found around nettles in field margins, hedgerows, and sunny woodlands and gardens.

Feeding Caterpillar feeds on nettle leaves; adult on nectar-rich buddleia, forget-me-not, bramble, and thyme.

Breeding Adults come out of hibernation and lay eggs. New adults emerge in June and lay eggs that hatch in late summer, overwintering as butterflies.

RED ADMIRAL
Vanessa atalanta

Size Caterpillar: up to 35mm (1⅜in); adult wingspan: 67–75mm (2⅝–3in).

ID features Butterfly has black wings, each with a red band; upper wings have white dots. Black caterpillar with white spots and pale spines.

Habitat Most flower-rich habitats, including gardens.

Feeding Caterpillar feeds on nettle leaves; adult on nectar-rich buddleia, ivy flowers, and rotting fruit.

Breeding Migrates to British Isles from spring, and may overwinter as an adult. Seen from March to November. Lays eggs in spring; new adults emerge in July.

Black band on each wing ....

Grey dot on wing ....

SMALL WHITE
Pieris rapae

Size Caterpillar: up to 25mm (1in); adult wingspan: 40–55mm (1½–2⅛in).

ID features Butterfly has white wings with small black tips. Male has a single dot on each fore wing, female has two. Blue-green caterpillar with a thin yellow stripe.

Habitat Gardens, allotments, hedgerows, farmland.

Feeding Caterpillar feeds on leaves of brassica family; adults on buddleia, teasel, nasturtiums, and lavender.

Breeding Two broods of eggs are laid each summer, with the pupae of the second brood overwintering.

ORANGE-TIP
Anthocharis cardamines

Size Caterpillar: up to 30mm (1¼in); adult wingspan: 40–52mm (1½–2in).

ID features Male butterfly has bright orange wing tips, female has black wing tips. Underwings of male and female are mottled green. Caterpillar is green fading to white down the sides.

Habitat Often seen in woods, damp areas such as pond margins, wetlands, and grasslands.

Feeding Caterpillar feeds on leaves of garlic mustard, lady's smock, and other brassicas; adult on nectar of spring-flowering brassicas, buttercups, red campion.

Breeding Adults emerge from March to June. They lay eggs and the pupae overwinter.

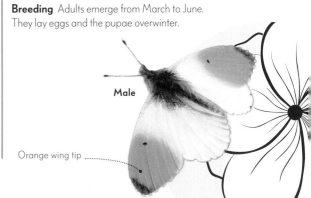

Male

Orange wing tip ....

..... Long
proboscis

HUMMINGBIRD HAWK-MOTH
Macroglossum stellatarum

Size Caterpillar: up to 60mm (2½in); adult wingspan: 50–58mm (2–2½in).

ID features Moth has a grey body with orange/brown hind wings, prominent antennae, and a long proboscis. Day-flying, similar to a hummingbird. Caterpillar is bright green with a yellow line on each side and a horn-like tail.

Habitat Varied, including gardens and urban parks.

Feeding Caterpillar feeds on hedge bedstraw, lady's bedstraw, and wild madder; adult on nectar-rich flowers such as buddleia, red valerian, and lavender.

Breeding Migrates from southern Europe from April or May. Adults are mainly seen May to September. Caterpillars feed from June to October.

ELEPHANT HAWK-MOTH
Deilephila elpenor

Size Caterpillar: up to 85mm (3¾in); adult wingspan: 45–60mm (1¾–2½in).

ID features Moth is olive-green with bright pink bars on wings and body. Flies from dusk. Caterpillar is grey/green/brown with two huge black false eyes on its head.

Habitat Gardens, woodland edges, and rough grasslands.

Feeding Caterpillar feeds on willowherb and bedstraw; adult on tubular flowers such as honeysuckle and buddleia.

Breeding Caterpillars feed July to September, and overwinter as pupae. Adults are seen May to August.

CINNABAR MOTH
Tyria jacobaeae

Size Caterpillar: up to 30mm (1¼in); adult wingspan: 34–46mm (1⅜–1¾in).

ID features Moth has distinctive black fore wings, each with a red bar and two spots. Day- and night-flying. Caterpillar is bright with black and yellow banding. The vivid colours indicate to predators that it is poisonous to eat; it gets toxins from its foodplants.

Habitat Open grassland; anywhere with ragwort.

Feeding Caterpillar feeds on common ragwort and groundsel; adult on nectar-rich flowers.

Breeding Caterpillars feed from June to October then overwinter underground as pupae. Adults are seen between May and August.

LARGE YELLOW UNDERWING
Noctua pronuba

Size Caterpillar: up to 50mm (2in); adult wingspan: 42–52mm (1½–2in).

ID features Moth has long, narrow mainly red/brown or black/brown fore wings, distinctive yellow hind wings with a black outer margin. Night-flying. Green or brown caterpillar, with black dots on the sides of the back.

Habitat Open grassy lowland habitats and gardens.

Feeding Caterpillar feeds on many foodplants, including docks, marigolds, and foxgloves; adult on nectar-rich flowers.

Breeding Caterpillars feed from August to May. Adults are seen between May and November.

Yellow hind
wing ....

POPLAR HAWK-MOTH
Laothoe populi

Size Caterpillar: up to 70mm (2¾in); adult wingspan: 65–90mm (2⅝–3½in).

ID features Moth has unique wing shape resembling a dead leaf, with the hind wing held in front of the fore wing, grey with red/brown bands across the wings. Night-flying. Caterpillar is bright green with yellow slashes, and a horn-like tail.

Habitat Woodlands, parks, and gardens; also fens, heathlands and moorland.

Feeding Caterpillar feeds on poplar trees, white and grey willow; adult does not feed.

Breeding Caterpillars feed from June to October then overwinter as pupae. Adults are seen May to July.

SWALLOW-TAILED MOTH
Ourapteryx sambucaria

Size Caterpillar: up to 54mm (2¼in); adult wingspan: 44–60mm (1¾–2½in).

ID features Moth has pale yellow wings, with two dark lines over the fore wings and one line on the hind wings. Pointed tail on hind wing. Night-flying. Caterpillar is brown, resembling a twig.

Habitat Woodlands, hedgerows, parks, and gardens.

Feeding Caterpillar feeds on trees such as blackthorn, hawthorn, goat willow, elder, and horse chestnut; adult on nectar-rich plants such as honeysuckle.

Breeding Caterpillar stage from August to June. Adults are seen in July.

Fluffy body ....

DRINKER MOTH
Euthrix potatoria

Size Caterpillar: up to 70mm (2¾in); adult wingspan 42–70mm (1½–2¾in).

ID features Moth is very fluffy, male red/brown with yellow patches, female deep yellow to pale buff, dark red, or brown. Night-flying. Caterpillar is dark grey with gold speckles, white hair tufts on either side of the body, and black tufts along the back.

Habitat Grasslands, fens, marshes, open woodlands; may occur in drier habitats such as gardens.

Feeding Caterpillar feeds upon various grasses and sedges, including common reed; adult does not feed.

Breeding Caterpillars feed from August to June. Adults are seen in July and August.

SIX-SPOT BURNET
Zygaena filipendulae

Size Caterpillar: up to 22mm (¾in); adult wingspan: 30–38mm (1¼–1½in).

ID features Moth has striking black wings with six bright red spots on each fore wing, and largely red hind wings. Day-flying. Caterpillar is yellow with black dots on each bump on its back.

Habitat Varied, including flowery grasslands, cliff-edges, woodland rides, and sand dunes.

Feeding Caterpillar feeds on common bird's-foot trefoil and occasionally greater bird's-foot trefoil. Adult feeds on nectar-rich plants such as thistles and other grassland flowers.

Breeding Caterpillars feed from August to June and may overwinter a second time. Adults are seen between June and August.

Red spots on wing ....

Shared spot
over both wings

SEVEN-SPOT LADYBIRD
Coccinella septempunctata

Size 6–7mm (¼in) long.

ID features Bright red wing casings, each with three black spots, and a shared spot over both wings. Body is black. Two white eye spots on the front of the head, with two white spots on the top of the black upper body.

Habitat Gardens, meadows, parks, hedgerows.

Feeding Adults and larvae eat small insects such as aphids.

Breeding Mainly seen between March and October. Mates in spring, larvae emerge as adults in September, overwinter in leaf litter, gorse, dead foliage.

COMMON EARWIG
Forficula auricularia

Size 10–15mm (½–⅝in) long.

ID features Brown-black with yellow legs and two long cerci (pincers) on the rear; male has curved cerci and female has straight. Short wing cases leave much of segmented body exposed.

Habitat Gardens, woodlands, and parks; prefers stones, wood, compost, and anywhere that is damp and dark.

Feeding Voracious garden hunters, eating mites, aphids, nematodes, and insect larvae. Also eats organic matter such as decaying leaves and vegetables in compost.

Breeding Seen all year round. Mates in autumn; females look after eggs until they hatch in spring.

GREEN LACEWING
Chrysoperla carnea

Size 10–15mm (½–⅝in) long.

ID features Lime green body. Wings are very delicate, translucent, and veined, similar to lace in appearance, hence the name.

Habitat Abundant in gardens, parks, and woodlands where aphids are most common.

Feeding Adults and young both feed on aphids. Ruthless hunters, once they have sucked all the juices out of an aphid, some lacewing larvae will use the dried-out body as camouflage, attaching the aphid skin to their own backs to hunt more aphids.

Breeding Seen on the wing from April to October. Female lays eggs on a hardened, mucus-like thread, which is attached to a leaf and suspended in the air. Adults emerge in midsummer and lay eggs; the adults from this brood hibernate until the following spring.

COMMON DARTER DRAGONFLY
Sympetrum striolatum

Size 38–43mm (1½–1¾in) long.

ID features Male is red with yellow patches on the sides of the upper body; female is golden brown with pale green upper body. Larvae (known as nymphs) are brown with six legs and a slightly spider-like body shape.

Habitat Ponds, and other still pools, including garden ponds. Occasionally away from water.

Feeding Perches and hovers around water bodies looking for insects; it darts forward to capture its prey.

Breeding Seen on the wing July to October (May to December in milder climates). Mates in summer. Larvae live in water for 11 to 12 months before emerging as adults.

Powerful wings

BLUE-TAILED DAMSELFLY
Ischnura elegans

Size 30–34mm (1¼–1⅜in) long.

ID features Black body with a light blue band towards the end, blue eyes, and blue upper body markings. One of the most common damselflies in Europe.

Habitat Very common near ponds and other water bodies, including boggy habitats, streams, and lakes.

Feeding Hunts around water for small insects such as midges and mosquitoes. Larvae feed on other aquatic larvae, flatworms, and bloodworms.

Breeding On the wing April to September. Female lays eggs in boggy marshland areas. When larvae are ready to moult, they emerge from water on to plants, leaving their skin behind.

WASP
Vespula spp.

Size Worker (female) and male: 12–17mm (⅝in); queen: 20–25mm (¾–1in) long.

ID features Black and yellow striped body with a narrow waist between upper body and abdomen. Each species of wasp can be identified by its facial pattern.

Habitat Varied, mainly gardens, parks, and woodlands.

Feeding Nectar-rich flowers such as sunflower, lavender, and others. Also eat rotten fruit. Adults catch insects and feed them to young wasps.

Breeding Queen emerges from hibernation in early spring and starts a nest. The new workers build a larger nest for the growing colony. The old queen and colony die in autumn, while a new queen overwinters.

Narrow waist ......

Cross-shaped markings ......

GARDEN SPIDER
Araneus diadematus

Size Male: 4–8mm (⅛–⅜in); female: 10–18mm (½–⅝in) body length.

ID features Colours vary between dark grey, brown, orange, and even yellow; five dots in the centre of the abdomen form a cross. Female usually seen upside down in the middle of her web.

Habitat Hedgerows, woodlands, and gardens.

Feeding Catches flying insects such as butterflies, flies, and even wasps in its sticky web.

Breeding Most active between June and October. Female lays eggs in a cocoon which she protects until her death in late autumn. Spiderlings hatch the following spring.

WOLF SPIDER
Pardosa spp.

Size Male: up to 6mm (¼in); female: up to 8mm (⅜in) body length.

ID features Dark brown, often with a pale stripe down the abdomen, and sometimes dark bands on the legs.

Habitat Leaf litter, woodlands, and gardens.

Feeding Does not create a web, instead chases down its insect prey.

Breeding Primarily seen between March and August. Female may live for several years.

Stripe on ...... abdomen

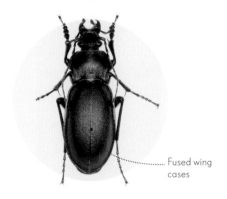

...... Fused wing
cases

VIOLET GROUND BEETLE
Carabus violaceus

Size 20–30mm (¾–1¼in) long.

ID features Large beetle with a violet sheen on its back and head; a very flat body shape, with wing cases fused together. Nocturnal and does not fly.

Habitat Fields, woodlands, and gardens; rests under logs, stones, and leaf litter during the day.

Feeding Hunts slugs, snails, and grubs such as beetle larvae and leatherjackets.

Breeding Primarily seen March to October.

RED SOLDIER BEETLE
Rhagonycha fulva

Size 7–10mm (¼–½in) long.

ID features Orange-red wing casings with black tips. Long, black, thread-like antennae.

Habitat Flowers, woodlands, and gardens.

Feeding Adult eats pollen and nectar, and insects such as aphids; larvae eat ground-dwelling invertebrates.

Breeding Seen between May and July, often as mating pairs on flower heads.

Antler-like jaws ......

STAG BEETLE
Lucanus cervus

Size Male: 35–75mm (1⅜–3in); female: 28–45mm (1–1¾in) long.

ID features Large jaws of male resemble antlers, hence its name. Body is dark brown, and reddish-brown in places, especially the antlers. Female similar but with smaller head and jaws.

Habitat Woods, parks, and often in gardens.

Feeding Larvae feed on decaying wood such as tree stumps, fallen trees, and roots; they need a large amount of food to survive into adult stage.

Breeding Seen between May and August. Males display their huge jaws to attract females, and duel with rivals. Larvae can take up to 6 years to become adults, which live only to mate and lay eggs in decaying wood.

DARK BUSH-CRICKET
Pholidoptera griseoaptera

Size 10–20mm (½–¾in) long.

ID features Dark brown-red body and legs, with paler patches along the top of the upper body, and yellow-green on the belly. Almost wingless; has very long antennae. Call is a noisy chirrup. One of the most common bush-crickets across Europe.

Habitat Abundant in gardens, parks, and woodland edges.

Feeding Mainly flowers, seeds, leaves, fruits; also insect larvae and aphids. Spends time in bramble patches.

Breeding Females lay their eggs in late summer in rotting wood or bark crevices with the young emerging 18 months later.

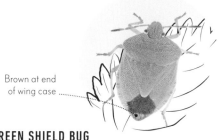

Brown at end of wing case ....

GREEN SHIELD BUG
Palomena prasina

Size 13–15mm (½–⅝in) long.

ID features Bright green in colour with tiny black dots and brown ends to wing cases. Changes to a bronze-green in autumn.

Habitat Abundant in gardens, parks, and woodlands.

Feeding Sap of a wide range of shrubs, trees, and herbaceous plants.

Breeding Seen between May and November. Adults overwinter and emerge in spring, laying their eggs on the undersides of leaves, with the nymphs appearing in June, and new adults in early autumn.

SMALL BLACK ANT
Lasius niger

Size Worker (female) and male: 3–5mm (⅛–¼in); queen: 8–9mm (⅜in) long.

ID features Black or dark brown, in colonies in loose soil and under stones. Males and queens have clear wings.

Habitat Gardens, woodlands, pastures, urban areas.

Feeding Small insects and sugary substances such as nectar and rotting fruit. Colonies also tend to and protect aphids to feed on the sugary honeydew they produce.

Breeding Colonies mainly made up of female workers, which are sterile. Queens emerge in late summer to mate with males; the males die, and the females look for a nesting site in which they start a new colony. Lifespan around 3 to 4 years for a queen.

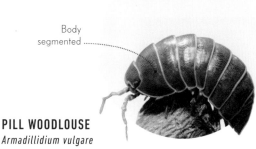

Body segmented ....

PILL WOODLOUSE
Armadillidium vulgare

Size Up to 18mm (¾in).

ID features Grey, often with yellow mottling; when threatened, will curl into a round ball.

Habitat Gardens, woodlands, and parks; damp and dark places under stones and logs.

Feeding Dead and decaying organic material, mostly of plant origin; young woodlice must eat faeces of adult woodlice to populate their digestive system with appropriate microbes.

Breeding Seen all year round.

STRIPED WOODLOUSE
Philoscia muscorum

Size Up to 11mm (½in) long.

ID features Grey and yellow, sometimes looking brown; yellow-beige around the edges of the body. Has two pointed projections at the rear called uropods.

Habitat Gardens and parks; damp and dark areas under stones and logs.

Feeding Dead and decaying organic material, mostly of plant origin; young woodlice must eat faeces of adult woodlice to populate their digestive system with appropriate microbes.

Breeding Seen all year round.

Yellow edges to body ....

..... Saddle

COMMON EARTHWORM
Lumbricus terrestris

Size 200–250mm (8–10in) long when extended.

ID features Brownish-purple above its bulbous, orange saddle, pinkish-yellow below.

Habitat In the soil, especially under lawns, and in dark, damp places under bags, bins, and log piles.

Feeding Prefers loose, mineral-rich soil with damp areas where it eats decaying leaves and other plant matter, drawing it down into the soil. Makes vertical burrows and comes to surface to feed.

Breeding After mating, produces a cocoon from which young worms emerge. Can live for 4 years or more.

GREEN EARTHWORM
Allolobophora chlorotica

Size 70–80mm (2¾–3in) long.

ID features Two variants, one pink-toned and the other green-yellow. The saddle has three pairs of sucker-like discs on the underside.

Habitat In the soil and in dark, damp locations such as beneath bags, bins, and log piles; prefers loose, mineral-rich soil with damp areas.

Feeding Decaying leaves and other plant matter. Makes horizontal burrows near the soil surface.

Breeding After mating, produces a cocoon from which young worms emerge. Lifespan is poorly known but likely to live for several years.

MILLIPEDE
Diplopoda

Size Up to 50mm (2in).

ID features Around 60 species known to occur in British Isles. Range from black to brown to grey, some with longitudinal stripes. Up to 60 body segments, each with 2 pairs of legs. When threatened, coils into a ball.

Habitat Gardens, leaf litter, woodlands; dark areas under stones and logs.

Feeding Eats dead plant matter. Some species eat living plants including roots such as potatoes.

Breeding Seen all year round. Females lay between 10–300 eggs which hatch after a few weeks. Lifespan is poorly known.

CENTIPEDE
Chilopoda

Size Up to 70mm (2¾in).

ID features A group of almost 60 UK species. Yellow to brown in colour with up to 80 segments, one pair of legs on each segment. Two rear legs are longer and used for feeling their surroundings.

Habitat Gardens, woodlands, and parks.

Feeding Eats invertebrates such as worms and insect larvae in leaf litter. Some species are herbivores, feeding on plant matter.

Breeding Seen all year round. Breeding habits variable depending on species. Can live between 5 and 6 years.

..... Long antennae

Brown bands ....

LEOPARD SLUG
Limax maximus

Size Up to 190mm (7½in) long.

ID features Primarily grey-brown, usually with leopard-like spots on its body; has a thick mantle on the rear of its head to protect its organs.

Habitat Gardens, woodlands, and parks.

Feeding A decomposer, feeding on mould growing on decaying logs; also thrives in dead organic matter and will eat carrion when available.

Breeding Seen all year round. Lays eggs in a cluster. Can live up to 3 years.

BLACK SLUG
Arion ater

Size 100–150mm (4–6in) long.

ID features Usually black, though it can be brick-red, orange, or grey, with long body. Has a thickened mantle on the rear of its head to protect its organs.

Habitat Gardens, woodlands, and parks; damp and dark areas under stones and logs.

Feeding A decomposer, feeding on fungi and dead plant matter, carrion, earthworms, and dung.

Breeding Seen all year round. Lays eggs in a cluster. Can live up to 2 years.

BANDED SNAIL
Cepaea nemoralis

Size Shell up to 20mm (¾in) in diameter.

ID features Colour variable, but majority have a light yellow, pinkish, or light brown shell with up to 5 dark brown bands running around the whorled shell; the enlarged lip of the shell is dark brown. Grey/light brown body.

Habitat Hedgerows, gardens, compost heaps, and near edges of fields.

Feeding Dead or decaying leaves, fungi, and moss, and fresh leaves of a variety of plants.

Breeding Seen between March and October with many hibernating through the winter. Lays clusters of eggs. Lives for about 6 years.

COMMON GARDEN SNAIL
Cornu aspersum

Size Shell up to 45mm (1¾in) in diameter.

ID features Grey body and a light brown shell with darker spiral bands, broken by irregular paler markings.

Habitat Hedgerows, gardens, and fields; found especially around areas of human habitation.

Feeding Decaying leaves and other plant matter such as vegetables and flowers.

Breeding Active all year except in very cold or dry weather. Lays eggs in clusters. Lives up to 4 years.

Paler markings
on shell ....

REPTILES AND
AMPHIBIANS

REPTILES AND AMPHIBIANS

Reptiles, including lizards and the occasional snake or slow worm, and amphibians, such as frogs, toads, and newts, visit gardens that have plenty of places for them to hide. Amphibians need boggy areas and water in which to breed, while reptiles prefer to bask on warm soil or rocks. Both look for a location full of insects and invertebrates for them to hunt.

The UK's largest snake, the grass snake is often seen near water or swimming in ponds; it poses no threat to humans.

Grass snake

Slow worm

Rocks retain heat, so they are used by reptiles to bask in the sun. Most species enjoy sitting on top of rocks, but slow worms love to gather heat from the humid areas underneath.

Compost heaps attract slow worms, which enjoy the warmth and eat the invertebrates that live there. Grass snakes may lay their eggs in compost heaps.

Water attracts grass snakes, which swim and hunt for prey. Grass snakes are seen relatively often in garden ponds looking for their next meal.

Thick vegetation offers a refuge for species such as adders and grass snakes. They bask in the open but dart to cover if they need to. Gorse, lavender, and heather all offer flowers that attract insects for reptiles to hunt, and bare lower stems under which they can bask.

Logs in a sunny spot make a suitable basking place for lizards, which also hunt for the insects and invertebrates that shelter there.

Common lizard

Adder

WHERE TO FIND REPTILES

Because they are cold-blooded, reptiles seek out areas that will retain heat for them to bask in.

Reptiles are mainly seen between March and October when the sun packs more of a punch. They often rest in the day and hunt in the evening and at night. In your garden you are most likely to see common lizards, grass snakes, and slow worms – and, occasionally, adders (see below) may visit gardens too.

During the cooler winter months, reptiles hibernate in compost heaps, loose soil, or even under garden sheds or decking. They're often very well hidden and are difficult to spot as they sense vibrations and escape quickly, usually before we are able to see them.

REPTILES IN YOUR GARDEN

As with any wildlife, we must respect reptiles if we are to share our space with them. Reptiles will not go out of their way to harm us but they do have teeth, and adders are venomous (the UK's only venomous reptile). With this in mind, the best way to observe them is from a safe distance. Be aware of areas where they may bask or hunt. Either avoid walking through the area, or make a noise as you approach so they can escape. If you need to lift something that you think a snake or slow worm may be underneath, use a long pole such as a broom handle.

WHERE TO FIND AMPHIBIANS

Like reptiles, amphibians rely upon the environment to source their heat, but they are able to spend time on land and in water.

Amphibians do not need such warm conditions as reptiles. They tend to be slower moving, and dwell in cooler and damper places. In gardens, we may see various species of frogs, toads, and newts, and they often move around in the evenings rather than in the direct heat of the day. They are able to absorb oxygen through their skin so they can survive underwater and even under ice to an extent, if there is sufficient oxygen in the water. They also have lungs, which enable them to spend time on land. When hibernating, amphibians can shelter under logs or leaves in a safe location, or amid pond vegetation.

There are several stages in an amphibian's lifecycle. Eggs (spawn) hatch into larvae (known as tadpoles in the case of frogs and toads) in water. Once the larvae absorb their tails, grow legs, and develop lungs (after about 14 weeks), they can live on land and in water as they grow to adulthood.

In water

Amphibians aren't fussy creatures and some species such as frogs will be found in the smallest of ponds and ditches looking to lay frog spawn. With their long back legs, frogs are much more adapted to swimming and hunting in deeper water than toads are. Both will shelter amid leaves of pond plants. if there is adequate vegetation newts, such as this great crested newt (right), and tadpoles will also have areas to thrive.

In wet habitats

Around water in boggy areas and wetlands, or simply in damp areas of the garden, there will be enough water for amphibians. Bog plants and mosses retain the sun's heat, and toads (left) and frogs will sit in this damp environment. These habitats also provide walkways for newts; since they are unable to jump like frogs and toads, newts need cover to leave the pond in search of food.

Under stones

It may not seem like the ideal habitat, but frogs (left) and toads both love to nestle beneath stones and rocks, which retain heat and provide moisture from the soil below. Great crested newts are also perfectly comfortable with exploring their surroundings and finding stones to hide under.

Around logs

Whereas reptiles love to bask on logs, amphibians prefer to live around the logs, with many such as newts (left) and toads enjoying the damp and dark decaying matter under and within log piles, and feeding on invertebrates that they find there.

FOOD AND PREDATION

Both reptiles and amphibians feed on similar foods:
mainly insects and other invertebrates. Even the
smallest fly is a source of nourishment.

Amphibians hunt on land and in water, whereas reptiles hunt only on land, and are faster to dart out and catch their prey. Newts are ruthless hunters, with their "vomerine teeth" – sharp projections in their jaw plates which they use to hold their prey. They have been known to shake snails out of their shells. Frogs and toads also have these teeth, as well as sticky tongues that they use to catch insects. Frogs, toads, and newts only feed every two or three days, although young amphibians feed daily on plankton and algae in the water. Snakes typically eat once a week if they find a large meal, or more often if the prey is smaller. The best way to attract all these species is to provide the right conditions in your garden for them to hunt naturally for food.

Insects and invertebrates

Frogs and toads feast upon flies out of the water, and eat other insects such as dragonflies, damselflies, and aquatic insects and their larvae. Lizards catch flies and bush-crickets among the garden vegetation. Lizards, frogs, newts, and toads hunt for slugs and snails, providing the perfect anti-slug solution in a wild garden. Slow worms also eat slugs, snails, spiders, and earthworms.

A common frog feasting on an earthworm.

Amphibians, reptiles, and small mammals

Grass snakes hunt for toads and frogs within a pond and are quite nimble when it comes to slithering their way through water looking for their prey. Newts also hunt tadpoles and spawn in the pond, and will occasionally take young newts. Adders are fearsome hunters and feed upon mice and voles in vegetation and bracken. They have pointed fangs at the front of their mouths from where they produce venom to help paralyze their prey.

A toad makes a large meal for a grass snake.

Mice are common prey of adders.

MAKING A
WATER HABITAT

Adding more water into your garden, or adapting an existing pond, will attract amphibians, reptiles, and aquatic life as well as a range of other wildlife.

Water is paramount for amphibians to survive as it's where the breeding part of their lifecycle takes place. Some reptiles rely upon water as a hunting ground for food. There is a range of ways we can use water to both attract and nourish reptiles and amphibians.

The most obvious water habitat that gardeners can provide is a pond, adapted to prioritize the needs of wildlife (see right). Boggy areas – either beside the pond or elsewhere in the garden – also offer a vital amphibian habitat. Even smaller, paved-over gardens can provide a water habitat with a container pond; just make sure to add stones or pieces of wood inside and out to create sloped sides for access.

Avoid pumps or fountains, as these will disturb pond life and deter amphibians, which need still, safe water in order to breed. Never use chemical pond treatments: frogs absorb oxygen from the water through their skins, and any chemicals you add will be absorbed by them, too. You may need to remove excess leaves and green blanketweed by hand or using a stick, avoiding times when spawn and tadpoles are in the pond. Do not introduce fish, as they may eat amphibians and invertebrates.

A good balance of water plants helps to keep the pond healthy and offers natural shelter under leaves as well as homes on the surface. For pond plant ideas, see pp.96–97.

This healthy-looking pond has a mix of plants at the margins as well as floating leaves in the centre. Stones at the edges offer easy access for reptiles.

WILDLIFE POND MUST-HAVES

Small adjustments to a pond will make it more suitable for reptiles and amphibians. Although frogs and toads are known to be jumpers, other amphibians need easy ways to access the water. Edges with shallow areas softened with plants will provide shelter and cover, while longer grass and boggy areas near ponds extend the habitat.

Sloped sides

Provide a ramp with stones, soil, or some broken terracotta to allow grass snakes and newts to access the pond. Some rocks around the edge in a sunny area will give a basking spot for reptiles.

Shallow areas

Make sure your pond has shallow areas. As well as providing access, the water here will be warmer, ideal for spawn, tadpoles, and larvae. They can feed on the algae that grows in the warmth.

Variety of vegetation

Include a good mixture of vegetation in the water for newts, tadpoles, and other pond life such as fly larvae and water beetles to hide among, providing food for amphibians within the water (see pp.96–97).

Boggy areas

Make a depression in the ground and place pond liner over it, then fill with soil and bog plants (see p.96). This area will stay moist and warm for reptiles and amphibians. Water it if it's dry.

PLANTING FOR PONDS

Ponds are ecosystems in themselves. A variety of pond plants will keep your pond healthy.

A balance of plants provides oxygen-rich water and spaces for species at different stages in their lifecycle to thrive. Pond plants are categorized by their planting depth and their function and location in the pond. Aim to have one- to two-thirds of the surface covered by plants (this will change with the seasons), including at least one floating plant to provide cover for amphibians while allowing sunlight to reach the bottom of the pond. This coverage will prevent the water heating up too much, which encourages algae. An excess of algae can remove oxygen and smother plants.

Nectar-rich flower spikes attract pollinators

Purple loosestrife

AVOIDING INVASIVE PLANTS

Choose pond plants carefully. Avoid invasive species that spread quickly and are hard to remove. If your pond begins to look swamped by plants, then cut back some of your plants, placing the cut off vegetation on the pond edge for a while so any trapped creatures can escape back into the water. The plant matter can then be composted.

Bog plants

These thrive around the edge of a pond (or in a bog garden), in wet conditions. They offer cover for amphibians entering or leaving the pond, and attract pollinators for reptiles and amphibians to hunt. Examples include:
- Creeping Jenny (*Lysimachia nummularia*)
- Cardinal flower (*Lobelia cardinalis*)
- Blue flag iris (*Iris versicolor*)
- Purple loosestrife (*Lythrum salicaria*)
- Sphagnum moss (*Sphagnum* spp.)

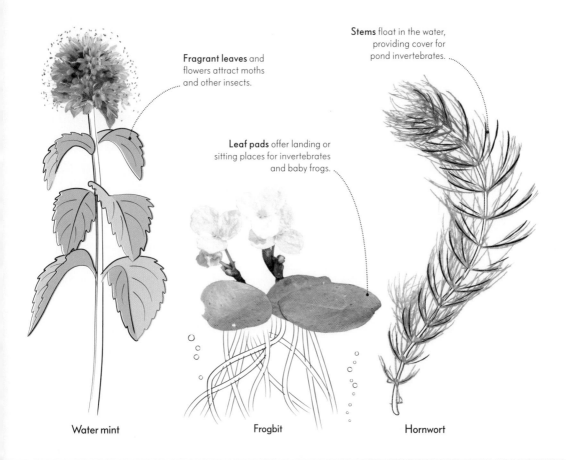

Fragrant leaves and flowers attract moths and other insects.

Stems float in the water, providing cover for pond invertebrates.

Leaf pads offer landing or sitting places for invertebrates and baby frogs.

Water mint

Frogbit

Hornwort

Marginals

With their roots in the water, marginals grow at the pond's edge, giving it a natural outline. They offer shelter and a space to feed for tadpoles and other larvae, and spawn and eggs thrive in the shallow water by their stems. Examples include:

- Pickerel (*Pontederia cordata*)
- Marsh marigold (*Caltha palustris*)
- Water mint (*Mentha aquatica*)

Floating plants

These plants root in the deep areas of a pond and have leaves and flowers on the surface. They offer shelter to pond creatures under the water, and shade so that the water does not heat up too quickly. Examples include:

- Frogbit (*Hydrocharis morsus-ranae*)
- Common water crowfoot (*Ranunculus aquatilis*)

Oxygenating and deepwater plants

These live under the surface and float or root loosely at the bottom. They give out high levels of oxygen, enabling plants, invertebrates, and amphibians to live underwater. Examples include:

- Common water starwort (*Callitriche stagnalis*)
- Hornwort (*Ceratophyllum demersum*)

SHELTER AND HABITATS

Garden buildings offer refuge for some reptiles and amphibians, and you can also add specially made "homes" for extra habitat.

Amphibians often seek out cool, damp spaces where they can rest during the day, leaving them at night in order to hunt. Outbuildings, such as sheds, are therefore an ideal habitat for these creatures. When entering a shed and moving items about, take care not to disturb any creatures who may be sharing your space. Reptiles seek shelter with warmth to give them energy to hunt in the daytime.

You can also buy or make a shelter to encourage more reptiles and amphibians with a purpose-built home. The ultimate winter retreat for reptiles and amphibians is a hibernaculum, an underground space that provides an overwintering habitat for wildlife. If you have space, it's a valuable garden addition (see pp.100–101).

Compost bins

Making your own compost is a vital part of making a wildlife-friendly garden (see p.40). The conditions in a compost bin are warm, damp, and dark – a great location for amphibians and reptiles such as snakes and slow worms to rest in the day and overwinter. To avoid harming these creatures, use blunt tools such as plastic spades instead of sharp steel tools, and turn your heap gently. Avoid turning it in summer to early autumn as there may be grass snake eggs in the heap.

Reptile mats

This is simply a metal sheet or piece of sturdy fabric such as a tarpaulin that warms up and provides a dark space underneath. Slow worms, grass snakes (left), adders, newts, frogs, toads, and even some small mammals will use the underneath of a reptile mat to keep warm while lizards will use the top as their basking spot. Consider your surroundings before selecting your preferred reptile mat as metal can be dangerous around dry areas; opt for using the fabric mat instead.

Frog and toad home

A small house made of wood or ceramic, and positioned by a damp area, will provide a space for reptiles and amphibians to shelter within. There are manufactured versions, basically terracotta igloos that balloon at the sides, providing plenty of space. A tile in the corner of a raised bed will provide similar shelter. The attraction of these homes is that they retain heat and moisture; a little vegetation or soil inside makes them more appealing.

ADDING FOOD NEAR SHELTER

Reptiles and amphibians will follow the food. So if you wish to entice more into your garden and are providing shelter specifically for these creatures, make sure to add plants nearby to attract insects. The combination of extra cover to enable the reptiles and amphibians to reach the shelter in safety, and insects feeding on the plants you have provided, makes a rich habitat.

MAKE A HIBERNACULUM

A hibernaculum is a place for hibernation. For reptiles and amphibians, a mix of rocks and logs with access points mimics crevices found in nature, offering safe and varied refuge.

Locate a spot in your garden, in an area that won't be disturbed in the winter. A good site would be one where you already see reptiles and amphibians, near some shrubs in a quiet corner with access to a grassy area. A mixture of sun and shade throughout the day is ideal.

YOU WILL NEED

- Safety gloves
- Spade
- Logs, branches, bricks, and rocks
- Drainpipe or plastic pipes about 1m (3ft) long; roughen up the inside of the pipes with sandpaper for reptiles and amphibians to climb though.

CARING FOR A HIBERNACULUM

In many ways, the best management for a hibernaculum is to leave it alone. Cut the grass and flowers on top of the hibernaculum once or twice at most each year, and always with care in case there are animals in the grass. You are aiming to create a natural, tussocky, rough surface that will be more interesting for reptiles and amphibians. Avoid stepping on the mound of the hibernaculum as this will press down on the buried logs, bricks, and other items, compressing some of the all-important nooks and crannies that are hibernation locations. Mice may use the hibernaculum over time, while bumblebees may burrow in the grassy top.

1. Dig a hole
Clear an area, then dig a hole about 50cm (20in) deep and around 1.5m (5ft) across, or smaller – working with the space you have available.

2. Fill the hole with logs and rocks

Fill the hole with logs, branches, bricks, rocks, allowing space in between these for reptiles and amphibians to pass through.

3. Insert tubes for access

Add a drainpipe on either side of the hibernaculum at ground level to give ways into and out of the hibernaculum.

4. Add soil

Now cover the pile with soil loosely between the materials and mounded to about 40cm (16in) high. Don't cover the entrance holes.

5. Sow or turf the top

You can turf the top for quick results, or sow it with wildflower seeds, which will provide food for pollinators in summer. Avoid compacting the soil.

POND DIPPING

Ponds contain more than amphibians and their young. They are often teeming with tiny invertebrates that are an important part of the ecosystem but too small to see in situ.

To watch wildlife thriving in a water source you have created is pure enjoyment. Many of us have had a go at pond dipping at some point in our lives, perhaps during school or with family. It's a great way to get to know some of your smaller garden residents. Simply put, pond dipping is a way of studying the smallest creatures in your pond, including spawn, tadpoles and larvae, by briefly transferring them to a tray of water where they can be better observed. The ideal time to pond dip is between March and October, when wildlife is generally active. Fewer creatures will be seen in winter.

It's worth dipping in different parts of the pond, including the shallows and planted-up areas (see p.95), as well as the deepest point to find a variety of species. At the bottom, you're most likely to find detritivores such as water hoglice, leeches, and flatworms. The mid-level holds the prime predators such as diving beetles, and dragonfly and damselfly larvae. Newts, frogs, and larger diving beetles may be in the vegetation. Tadpoles stick to the edges of the pond. If you pond dip several times over the spring and summer you may be able to see pond creatures at various stages in their lifecycle.

Many pond creatures hide in vegetation when we are near. Gently taking them out to observe allows us to take a closer look at species such as this smooth newt.

HOW TO POND DIP

1. Gather your creatures

You only need a net and some trays to pond dip. Pale-coloured trays allow you to see the creatures more clearly. Fill the trays with pond water. Use a net to scoop out some water creatures from an area of the pond and quickly turn out the net into a tray. Try to separate predators and prey into different trays.

2. Look closely

Once you've placed your creatures in the tray, use a magnifying glass or microscope to work out the family you are looking at and then try to work out the species. To use your microscope, add a pot underneath with the creature and water inside and look through the eye-piece. You can purchase handheld devices, which are safer for wildlife. There are countless books and charts available to help identify your pond creatures, including within this book (see pp.108–109).

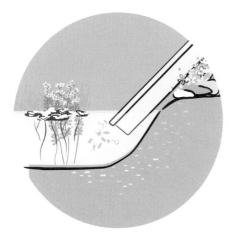

3. Return them to the water

Don't let the water and the creatures heat up in the sun. Identify them, or take a picture if you can, and gently let them back into the water where you found them.

Black spots on orange belly

GREAT CRESTED NEWT
Triturus cristatus

Size Adult: 15–17cm (6–6¾in) long.

ID features Breeding male is dark grey with black spots, jagged crest down the back, and a smooth crest with a silvery flash down the tail; belly is orange with black markings. Breeding female is similar, with no crest and tail flash, but with an orange stripe on the base of the tail. Non-breeders have no crest and more subdued colours; more likely to be seen on land. All have warty skin, unlike the smooth skin of other newts.

Habitat Breeds in ponds and slow-moving water. Outside breeding season prefers wet woodlands, hedgerows, marshes, and grasslands near its breeding site, and shelters in log piles and under reptile mats. Hibernates underground amid tree roots and stone walls.

Feeding Larva feeds on small water invertebrates such as water hoglouse and freshwater shrimp; eft (young newt with legs and lungs) hunts for small slugs on land. Adult newt looks for insects, slugs, and worms in gardens, and aquatic invertebrates and newt larvae in ponds.

Plants On land, lives among marshland vegetation, allowing it to keep damp as it moves and feeds. In the water, lives among marginal plants.

Breeding Seen March to October. Breeds March to June. Larvae emerge from eggs after 4 weeks, growing gills underwater and developing front legs first. Juveniles develop lungs around 10 weeks, after which they walk on land. After 4 months they metamorphose into adults, which can live for 16 years. They return to water to breed.

Note Great crested newts are a priority species in the UK; it's an offence to disturb them, their habitat, or their breeding cycle, or to capture or remove them.

SMOOTH NEWT
Lissotriton vulgaris

Size Adult: 7–11cm (2¾–4½in) long.

ID features Grey to brown body; has an orange belly with black spots all over in patterns individual to each newt. In the breeding season, male has a smooth crest running unbroken from shoulder to tail. Eft is light brown with speckles.

Habitat Breeds in ponds, coming out mainly during the non-breeding period, when it may be found in gardens, woodlands, hedgerows, and marshes with a water source nearby. Prefers boggy garden areas with dark, damp places for hibernating. Newts hibernate in log piles, under stones and piles of leaves, and in purpose-built hibernacula.

Feeding Larva mainly feeds on crustaceans, molluscs, and larvae of other amphibians in ponds. Adult eats insects, caterpillars, worms, and sometimes slugs in gardens.

Plants At water's edge, likes tall bog and marginal plants for shelter. In water, leaves of marginals offer shelter. Female lays eggs individually, each wrapped in a submerged leaf of an aquatic plant to protect it.

Breeding Seen March to October. Breeding between April and June. Larvae emerge from eggs after 4 weeks, growing their gills underwater and growing their front legs first. Juveniles develop lungs around 10 weeks, after which they are known as efts and can breathe and walk on land. After 4 months they metamorphose into adults, which can live to about 7 years of age.

COMMON FROG
Rana temporaria

Size Adult: 6–9cm (2½–3½in) long.

ID features Colour varies from a deep forest green to a rusty brown, to red or even dark yellow; variation seems to depend on the individual and the temperature rather than region. Has smooth skin and large eyes with circular pupils, and a dark patch behind each ear. Long back legs, with dark bands, extend beyond the rear of the body. Moves by hopping rather than walking. Tadpole is brown with paler speckles and pointed tail.

Habitat Breeds in ponds. Also found in wetlands and boggy habitats, including woodlands, hedgerows, and grasslands; hides in damp and dark areas before moving in the evening and at night when it's safer. Hibernates in garden log piles, under rocks, and purpose-built hibernacula. Uses frog houses in damp places or by ponds in gardens.

Feeding Tadpole feeds on algae and small water creatures such as daphnia. Adult and juvenile feed on insects such as flies that they catch with their tongues, and snails, slugs, and worms.

Plants Adult looks for vegetation to hide in, particularly tussocky plants on land. Tadpole shelters among marginal water plants.

Breeding Seen from February to October. Frog spawn is laid in clumps at the water's edge from around February to March, with tadpoles hatching in March. Tadpoles take about 14 weeks to lose their gills, absorb their tails, and grow legs, becoming juvenile frogs and able to leave the water and live on land. Adults can live for about 5 years.

COMMON TOAD
Bufo bufo

Size Adult: up to 10cm (4in) long.

ID features Brown to grey-brown; its skin has wart-like bumps down the back and sides. Eyes have horizontal pupils and copper-coloured irises. The back legs are short (compared to a frog). Instead of jumping like a common frog, it walks and is seen in spring crossing roads in the evening as it moves to or from breeding ponds. Tadpole is black with a rounded tip to its tail.

Habitat Can be seen in gardens, wet woodlands, hedgerows, and grasslands surrounding suitable wet habitats. Typically lurks among the foliage, resting during the day in boggy garden areas with dark, damp places; not often seen in ponds except when breeding, but will feed on the water's edge and in vegetation surrounding the pond. Will use a toad or frog house.

Feeding Adult primarily feeds on slugs, snails, and other smaller garden invertebrates but larger adults may try to eat juvenile slow worms, grass snakes, and small mice. Tadpole eats algae and small water creatures such as daphnia.

Plants Needs a mixture of marginal and bog-loving pond plants , and tussocky plants on land for cover.

Breeding Can be seen February to October. Toad spawn is present from around February to March; these long strings, containing two rows of eggs, can be seen wrapped around pieces of vegetation. Toads hatch after two weeks; tadpoles take around 14 weeks to lose their gills, absorb their tails, and grow legs, at which point they can leave the water and live on land. Adults can live up to 10 years.

...... Warty skin

Feet grip
smooth surfaces

COMMON LIZARD
Zootoca vivipara

Size Adult: 10–15cm (4–6in) long.

ID features Variable in colour, but typically brown-grey, or greenish, with rows of darker spots or stripes down the back and sides. Male has a bright yellow-orange underside with spots, while female has paler belly with no spots. May shed its tail when threatened so it can run away; the tail takes months to regrow.

Habitat Can be found in a huge range of habitats, including gardens, and on heathland, moorland, woodland, and grassland – anywhere with suitable crevices and basking areas. Will use reptile mat.

Feeding Small insects and invertebrates, such as flies, spiders, and even small snails around dry areas such as dry-stone walls and in gardens.

Plants Needs vegetation around its basking locations to scuttle into when startled.

Breeding Best seen between March to October. Adults produce three to eleven young in July, which mature around 2 years old. Hibernates between October and February, alone among leaf litter, crevices in rocks and fallen wood, and underground; relatively cold tolerant. Average lifespan 5 to 6 years.

SLOW WORM
Anguis fragilis

Size Adult: 40–50cm (16–20cm) long.

ID features Looks similar to a snake but smaller and, unlike a snake, has eyelids; it is in fact a legless lizard. Has smooth, grey skin; male is paler and sometimes has dull-blue spots, whereas female is larger with dark sides and often a black stripe down the spine.

Habitat Very commonly found in a range of habitats such as heathland, grassland, woodland; a frequent visitor to gardens even in urban environments. Will take to a purpose-made hibernaculum very easily. Also found in compost heaps and under garden waste bags or boxes where heat may be generated.

Feeding Feeds on slugs, snails, spiders, and earthworms.

Plants Prefers vegetation that will protect it when moving around, such as ferns, low shrubs, ground cover.

Breeding Best seen between March and October. Mating takes place in April to May and female gives birth to live young in late summer after incubating eggs internally. Hibernates between October and March in the base of trees, around rotting trees and discarded wood, in dense grass tussocks, and in disused small mammal burrows. Typical lifespan 10–20 years. Longest-lived of the lizards in the UK.

GRASS SNAKE
Natrix helvetica

Size Adult: 70–100cm (28–39in) long; largest garden reptile in Britain.

ID features A dark forest-green with small black bars across the body from head to tail except across the back; colour varies across its European range, with some forms treated as closely related species. Has a yellow and black collar and a pale belly. Female typically larger than male.

Habitat Range of habitats, but prefers areas with adequate hiding locations and with small pools, such as heathland, grassland, woodland, and sometimes gardens. Enjoys basking spots in the sun with vegetation to hide in nearby.

Feeding Main prey are amphibians and fish, slugs on land. Also eats small mammals and reptiles plus other invertebrates. Often hunts in ponds.

Plants Uses vegetation in and around pond edges as hunting grounds.

Breeding Best seen between March and October. Female lays 10 to 40 eggs in dense, rotting vegetation such as compost heaps; they hatch in late summer to autumn. Average lifespan 15 to 25 years.

ADDER
Vipera berus

Size Adult: 40–80cm (16–32in) long.

ID features Unmistakable greyish snake with dark zig-zag pattern down the spine, often looking similar to a chequerboard with markings referred to as "diamonds". Male is mostly grey, while female is lighter or red-brown. Some local populations are black. Has bright red eyes with vertical pupils.

Habitat Mostly associated with heathland, it is also found in woodland, moorland, and scrub habitats, as well as in gardens especially those near to where it lives in the wild. Uses basking spots in gardens especially with bracken nearby, and can be seen peering back at you while coiled up in its basking spot. Will use underground burrows of small mammals for hibernating, or purpose-built hibernacula.

Feeding Feeds on small lizards and mammals, and chicks of ground-nesting birds. Adders are venomous snakes and will use their venom to kill their prey, following the weakening prey as the venom takes effect.

Plants Prefers dense vegetation where it can bask on bare ground in the open, with cover to retreat to. Plants such as gorse, ferns, bramble, heather, and bracken are all great habitats for adders to feel safe in a garden.

Breeding Best seen between March and October. Adders do not lay eggs, but female gives birth to up to 10 or 15 young in late summer or early autumn. Mating occurs in early spring when leaving hibernation; males perform a dance as they fight one another for females. Average lifespan 10 years, sometimes 15.

Note Whilst they are considered dangerous, adders are not aggressive and only retaliate when threatened, for example, being stepped on or picked up. Leave them alone and they will avoid you.

Distinctive zig-zag markings ....

Hind legs act as rudders

POND SKATER
Gerridae

Size Up to 15mm (⅝in) long.

ID features Brown/black, with 6 legs, the front pair to catch prey, the middle for propulsion, the hind pair for steering. Skims along the water surface. Uses its sharp mouthparts to feed. Numerous species across Europe.

Habitat Many different water bodies, such as garden ponds, streams, slow-moving rivers, lakes, and pools.

Feeding Catches small insects trapped on the water surface then feeds upon them, sucking out internal juices.

Breeding Seen between April and November. Eggs are laid in April with the young hatching soon after, the nymphs then go through 5 moults before reaching adult appearance and size.

WATER SPIDER
Argyroneta aquatica

Size 8–15mm (⅜–⅝in) body length.

ID features Lives underwater but is seen coming up to the surface to gather air between the hairs on its grey-brown body; it takes the air down to its web and lives in the air bubble. Sometimes referred to as "bell spider" due to its bell-shaped web made in underwater vegetation.

Habitat Heavily vegetated ponds, lakes, and slow-flowing streams and rivers. Needs water plants to create its web.

Air bubble

Feeding Eats other small invertebrates such as water hoglice, small damselfly larvae, and shrimps.

Breeding Seen all year round. Female builds a secluded egg chamber within submerged vegetation where she lays her eggs and stays to protect them. Eggs hatch after a few weeks and small spiders disperse into the water.

WATER HOGLOUSE
Asellus aquaticus

Size Up to 15mm (⅝in) long.

ID features Looks similar to woodlouse, brown with 14 legs and two gill plates at the rear, and two pairs of antennae, one short and one long.

Habitat Found in ponds and streams; capable of living in areas of low oxygen including in polluted waters.

Feeding Decaying matter at the bottom of the pond.

Breeding Seen all year round. Breeds in any vegetated pond in spring and summer. Female carries her eggs in a pouch under her body until they hatch.

GREAT DIVING BEETLE
Dytiscus marginalis

Size Around 30mm (1¼in) long.

ID features Very large, mainly black with a greenish sheen and a mustard border around the wing cases. Male is shiny whereas female has deep grooves down the wing cases. Larvae are light brown with biting jaws.

Habitat Ponds, slow-moving water, and even temporary pools that it finds during nocturnal flights. Needs vegetation within its water body as a hunting ground. Pupates in boggy soil beside water.

Feeding Hunts for a variety of small invertebrates, tadpoles, and fish in ponds.

Breeding Seen all year; larvae present in spring and summer. Female lays eggs in early spring into the stems of aquatic plants; the eggs take 18–20 days to hatch.

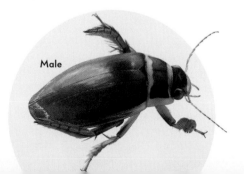

Male

COMMON FRESHWATER SHRIMP
Gammarus pulex

Size Up to 20mm (¾in) long.

ID features Grey or brown crustacean with a flattened body and a long, curving back. Has 7 pairs of legs and 2 pairs of antennae. In spring the larger male is often seen holding on to the smaller female.

Habitat Flowing water such as streams, pools, and rivers, under vegetation and stones. Often seen swimming on their sides or crawling on rocks in streams.

Feeding Detritus and dead organic matter including algae in ponds.

Breeding Female carries eggs in the body within a brood pouch, where the eggs hatch after 21 days. The young stay inside the brood pouch until the female moults. May live for 9–12 months.

FLATWORM
Turbellaria

Size Variable according to species; can be from 5mm (¼in) to 35mm (1⅜in) long.

ID features Brown, white, or black with long, slug-like, flattened body. At least 13 species of freshwater flatworm have been recorded in the British Isles.

Habitat On the bottom of ponds, lakes, streams, living among the decaying matter or in vegetation.

Feeding Many are predators of small invertebrates such as water mites and water fleas; some feed on decaying vegetation in the water body.

Breeding Can reproduce sexually or asexually depending on the species; regenerates after damage.

RAMSHORN SNAIL
Planorbarius corneus

Size Up to 35mm (1⅜in) in diameter.

ID features Shell can vary between shades of brown, auburn, and black, and coils in a flat spiral. Often seen attached to rocks or vegetation, or holding onto material on the water surface.

Habitat Ponds, slow-moving streams, and lakes; water with plenty of vegetation.

Feeding Feeds on algae by scraping its tongue on the surface on which the algae grow.

Breeding Can be seen all year; eggs are laid in protective masses of jelly on plants or rocks underwater.

POND SNAIL
Lymnaea stagnalis

Size Up to 50mm (2in) in height.

ID features Shell is black or brown, with a conical spire.

Habitat Well-vegetated, still or slow-moving water bodies; tolerant of pollution.

Feeding Scrapes its tongue on the surface on which algae grow.

Breeding Can be seen all year; eggs are found in protective masses of jelly on plants under the water.

Brown body

BIRDS

BIRDS

A constant presence in the garden, birds are most visible in winter when branches are bare and they are seeking food, and most audible in spring when they sing to stake a claim to their territory and attract a mate. They may nest in a garden, and many will readily come to bird feeders. By providing food and shelter for a variety of birds, we can encourage more to visit our gardens, where we can get a close-up look at how they behave and interact.

Tree sparrows (left) and house sparrows are declining in numbers, so offering suitable food and shelter in a garden helps to support the existing populations.

BIRDS THROUGH THE YEAR

Birds have a seasonal cycle of behaviour,
which is tied to their breeding patterns
and to the availability of food.

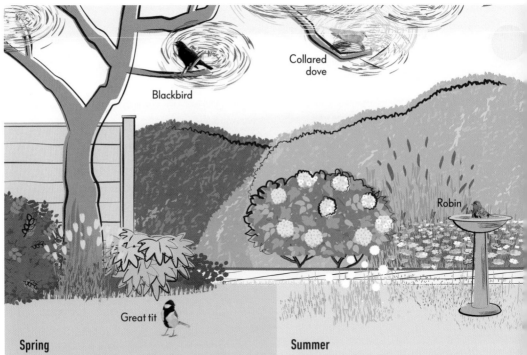

Blackbird

Collared dove

Robin

Great tit

Spring

Birdsong is the sound of spring. Birds sing at this time to attract a mate and sometimes to assert their territory. Other calls warn of danger, such as a predator nearby. Meanwhile, they are looking for nesting locations; thrushes, for example, nest in shrubs, finches at the tops of trees, and tits in tree holes. All can be seen gathering nesting material.

Summer

After hatching, growing their adult feathers, and fledging (leaving the nest), young birds sit near their parents, calling, with their wings shaking, looking for food. This coincides with an abundance of caterpillars and larvae, so the parents fly back and forth, gathering this food from plants and feeding it to their young.

Resident birds such as robins, blue tits, and blackbirds are in the garden all year. Migratory species visit for summer or winter. In summer chiffchaffs, blackcaps, swallows, and willow warblers arrive to breed, lured by the abundance of insects; in winter they fly south, often to Africa. In winter, siskins, redwings, and fieldfares travel from colder parts of Europe for the milder winter conditions and to feed on berries.

To make a garden as welcoming as possible, adapt your gardening activities to fit around aspects of bird behaviour. It's vital not to disturb birds while they are nesting (all wild birds, their eggs, and their nests are protected by law). Avoid cutting hedges between February and August. If you can leave your lawn or some patches of wildflowers to grow longer in late spring, there will be more insects for birds to feed on.

Redwing

Wren

Song thrush

Autumn

There is little birdsong apart from that of the robin, which sings all year to defend its territory. Young birds mature and some species migrate, while others arrive in search of berries. Sloes, blackberries, and hawthorn are some of the berries on offer for growing young birds and migrants such as redwings.

Winter

With little foliage on trees and shrubs, and a lack of food, this is when birds mostly rely on gardens. They look for shelter in trees and shrubs, and food from feeding stations, fruit, and invertebrates. Thrushes, long-tailed tits, and finches gather to feed and huddle for warmth when they roost for the night.

NATURAL FOOD SOURCES

The food that is naturally available is vital to birds' survival; the more we can provide in our gardens, the more birds will visit.

While putting up feeders (see pp.118–19) is a welcome supplement to garden birds' diet, natural sources are hugely important. In addition, some birds, such as dunnocks, chiffchaffs, or redwings, do not approach feeders, however hungry they are. A variety of plants – and the insects that feed on them – will provide a range of food for different bird species, giving a fairly consistent supply all year round.

Seeking out food

Birds feed at different levels in the garden depending on the species. Some larger birds, such as thrushes and pigeons, hop around at ground level looking for invertebrates and fallen seed. Blackbirds rely on their eyesight and hearing to locate worms in a lawn. The more agile tits are usually in the canopy of mid-level trees and shrubs in search of caterpillars. Tits and finches sometimes travel in flocks to make searching for food easier (and so that they can look out for predators while feeding). Small birds, such as wrens and dunnocks, stay at ground level sheltering and searching for food.

Plant food sources

Seed heads on plants such as thistle, poppy, and sunflower are full of nutritious seeds, which garden finches extract with their strong, slim beaks. Birds also feast on tree fruits and nuts,

Leaving seed heads on flowers over the winter provides food for seed-eating birds such as this goldfinch.

Lawns provide grubs and insects for birds such as this blackbird (left), thrushes, and robins.

including cherries, apples, hazelnuts, and acorns. If space is short for a tree in your garden, patio types are available, such as dwarf cherry. Berries enable birds to gain both nutrients, and water from their juices – vital in winter when the ground freezes and birds cannot hunt for worms or snails.

Prey food sources

Birds eat a variety of insects and invertebrates. Some forage on the ground for beetles, snails, and worms, while others such as woodpeckers and treecreepers reach into bark with their beaks for small insects. Swallows and swifts snatch flying insects from the air. In spring, as birds are feeding their young, they need soft food that can be broken down; caterpillars and larvae of other invertebrates are a key food at this time. Birds gather these from all sorts of plants, from trees to so-called "weeds" like nettles, which are caterpillar foodplants. By providing for the needs of insects and invertebrates (see pp.56–61) – introducing pollinator-friendly plants, leaving a patch of nettles to grow behind the shed, or creating a pond – you can in turn provide help to support your local bird population.

A rich source of natural food also encourages birds of prey, such as owls and sparrowhawks, as well as some birds in the crow family to visit larger gardens to catch small mammals, reptiles, amphibians, and other birds. A pond or rough grass is a great hunting ground for these birds.

Tawny owls (right) and other birds of prey hunt in gardens, especially in rural areas.

BIRD FEEDERS

Individual feeders or feeding stations provide food for a variety of species; tailor the feeders and food to the species you wish to attract.

Feeders are excellent in any size of garden even if space is limited or if you cannot plant for birds. You can hang single feeders or group them into a feeding station. Locate your feeders away from areas such as a washing line, or near a back door, where humans will cause disturbance.

To keep feeders protected from pets and other potential predators, place them near to cover where birds can fly to safety when alerted. If you add some thorny plants around the base of your feeders, this may also deter predators. You may find that small mammals come to feed on the spilled seed; if you want to discourage this, buy feeders with trays underneath to catch any waste.

Give feeders a good clean to help prevent the spread of diseases. The majority of feeders come apart. Submerge them in soapy water and scrub them with a nail brush or old toothbrush once a week.

Table feeder
This is often a sturdy wooden structure, but various designs are available, including tables suspended from trees. All types of food work well on them.

Mesh feeder
Ideal for peanuts and suet feeds that need to be broken apart, a mesh feeder attracts birds such as tits, finches, and woodpeckers, which grasp hold of the bars.

Tube feeder

Suitable for the majority of mixes, this feeder comes in a range of sizes with some having two holes and others having upwards of four, each with a perch just below the hole.

Suet ball feeder

Typically a long tube, this has large mesh squares to hold suet logs and suet balls. Rectangular feeders are available for suet blocks.

TYPES OF BIRD FOOD

Some basic bird foods are suitable to put out in feeders all year round. Others, such as peanuts and suet balls, offer fat and protein that are particularly useful in the winter months when food is scarce, or to build up energy before migration takes place.

Classic and high-energy mixes

The classic mix contains sunflower seeds and chopped nuts with oats and cereal. The high-energy mix (right) adds sunflower hearts and chopped peanuts with fewer "filler" elements.

Peanuts

Best offered in a feeder so that birds break them up as they feed, peanuts are particularly high in protein for extra energy.

Niger seeds

These tiny seeds are devoured by finches; because of their size they require a specialized feeder.

Suet balls

Made of fat with seeds and sometimes insects embedded in them, these are high energy.

WATER FOR BIRDS

In addition to providing water for drinking, a bird bath is a place for birds to clean themselves – and it may attract other wildlife.

Bathing in shallow water allows birds to dampen their feathers in readiness for preening, when they use their beak to remove any parasites, bacteria, and vegetation that may have accumulated during their adventures around the garden. A range of bird baths is available to suit different types of birds and to fit the outdoor space that you have. You can also make one with an adapted washing up bowl or shallow dish. Ensure your bath has gently sloping sides, so that small birds can find a suitable depth at which to bathe and preen themselves. If your bird bath doesn't have sloping sides, add stones in and around the bath to create a ramp.

Pond edges

If you have a garden pond, you can ensure that an area is suitable for birds to enter the pond so that they can bathe. Add a slope of stones of varying sizes to form a "beach" so that different sizes of birds can all walk into the water to their preferred depth.

Ground level

Baths at or near ground level are ideal for larger species such as thrushes, pigeons, and doves to bathe in, as they can easily walk into the water. Place the bath with cover such as shrubs nearby for species to retreat to, but not directly around

A shallow beach area at the edge of a pond allows both large and small birds to access the water.

Wood pigeon

Robin

LOOKING AFTER YOUR BIRD BATH

Keep your bird bath topped up with fresh water, especially in summer when birds may have few other water sources. Clean the bath regularly so that it remains safe and appealing. Empty it at least once a week, removing any debris such as fallen leaves and droppings. Give the outer rim a scrub with soap and water to remove bacteria and any build up of algae. Bacteria can spread disease among birds; algae isn't so harmful but can be slippery or clog the bird bath. Refill the bath with clean water.

In icy weather, add a tennis ball; it will move about enough to ensure the water doesn't ice over. Keep the water low in winter, no more than 5cm (2in), so that large and smaller species can access it easily.

the bath or predators may hide in it. A shallow bath is easy for smaller species to use as they can stand in the water and sit down to bathe. For a slightly deeper bath – over 5cm (2in) – a ramp or stones allows smaller creatures to climb in and out. Depending on the size of your ground-level bath, you may find that other creatures make use of the water – an opportunistic frog or toad, for instance. These baths can also be positioned on a wall or low table.

Raised plinth

A classic bird bath is a wide bowl on a metal or concrete plinth. These are ideal for smaller species that like to bathe together, such as sparrows or starlings, or for more cautious species, such as tits and wrens, that like to take a bath but need a quick escape route. They work well placed near to cover such as shrubs, climbers (ivy is perfect), or trees, and they make an attractive focus in borders.

Starlings

Song thrush

Larger birds such as this thrush can stand in a shallow bath to clean themselves. Smaller birds use pebbles in the bath to stand on.

Starlings (above) and sparrows are the birds that like to gather in groups for a splashy bath. A raised plinth allows them to look out for possible predators.

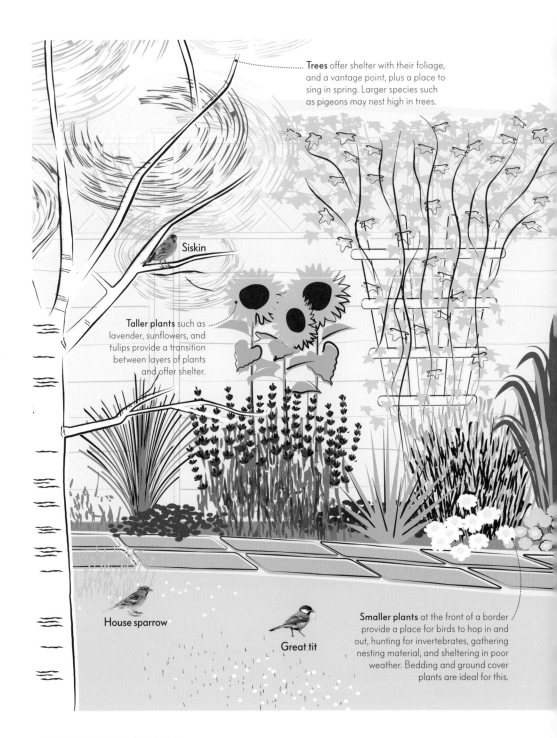

Trees offer shelter with their foliage, and a vantage point, plus a place to sing in spring. Larger species such as pigeons may nest high in trees.

Siskin

Taller plants such as lavender, sunflowers, and tulips provide a transition between layers of plants and offer shelter.

House sparrow

Great tit

Smaller plants at the front of a border provide a place for birds to hop in and out, hunting for invertebrates, gathering nesting material, and sheltering in poor weather. Bedding and ground cover plants are ideal for this.

Climbers fit into all but the smallest of spaces. Some, such as ivy and climbing hydrangea, are dense and offer shelter and nesting places for species such as wrens and thrushes.

Shrubs provide shelter when birds are foraging and visiting feeders, and birds may nest in larger shrubs. Place shrubs further into a border or against a fence.

Wren

Plants in containers from shrubs to annual flowering plants can be grouped together to give birds a refuge when startled. Most gardens can accommodate these smaller plants easily.

SHELTER AND NESTING

In spring, birds build nests to lay eggs and raise chicks. For the rest of the year, they roost in a location where they feel safe from predators.

Shrubs, climbers, and trees are fantastic natural shelter and nesting locations for birds. The more varied the plants, the better, to give birds more options – as well as more food sources. Evergreens such as laurels and camellias give year-round cover for nesting and roosting, but also for birds to dart into to escape a predator or shelter from a downpour. Dense shrubs such as cotoneaster offer good roosting potential and protection from predators. Climbers such as ivy are excellent cover and a source of nesting material. Taller trees provide a vantage point that larger birds may look for. If you plant your garden in layers (see pp.38–39) you will have a range of vegetation at all levels.

If you don't have the space for borders of plants, or if you are in rented accommodation or a paved garden, you can create a similar effect with containers on patios; birds may not nest there but there will be plenty of cover for birds to make use of for shelter. Smaller shrubs such as lavender are particularly good in containers as they are branching and can be dense, while their flowers are loved by pollinators. You can also find dwarf fruit trees such as apples, crab apples, and cherry, which will offer perching places for birds. Dunnocks, wrens, and other shyer birds enjoy the shelter provided by container plants.

NESTING BOXES

With the rapid loss of natural nesting places,
bird boxes are a vital addition to a wild garden
to maximize nesting and roosting opportunities.

Nest boxes aim to offer conditions similar to those that different species look for naturally; there are therefore a number of different types. Start by identifying the species that visit your garden and surrounding area, and find a suitable nest box for them – there's little point catering for species you're unlikely to attract. Avoid stained or treated wood, unless the stain or preservative is water-based and safe for birds.

Trees, fences, and garden walls are all good locations. As a guide, fix a nest box 1.5–2m (5–6½ft) above the ground. For a wall or fence, allow a 30cm (1ft) gap from the top so that cats can't reach down and push a paw into the box. Ideally choose a spot that faces northeast, to protect from the prevailing winds and rain, but if there is adequate cover, any direction is fine.

Nest boxes must not be disturbed at any point during the breeding season (roughly from March to September). Once the season is over, observe the box for a few days to check that there are no comings and goings. If it's empty, it's time to clean the box. Take it down and, wearing gloves, remove any discarded eggs or bodies of young chicks, and take out the nesting material. Scrub the box with hot water and leave it to dry. Put any clean material back in the box for birds to roost in winter, and dispose of the rest.

Holed nest boxes

The familiar nest boxes with a hole in the front are suitable for smaller garden birds, as the hole is too small for predator birds to enter. Choose one with a hole 26–30mm (1–1¼in) in diameter for birds such as blue tits and coal tits. Up to 35mm (1⅜in) in diameter will attract slightly larger birds such as great tits.

Open-fronted boxes

These boxes are great for species that create larger nests or like a vantage point. Robins, wrens, and wagtails take to these boxes when placed next to ivy and other climbers as they offer dense cover, which is their preferred habitat.

Specialist boxes

There is a huge variety of boxes catering to individual species, many of which struggle to find natural nesting sites. Sparrows may use holed nest boxes, but there are larger boxes that enable them to nest in communities. Swallows and martins nest in cups under house eaves, while swifts nest in boxes below the eaves.

Nesting boxes are available in many materials and variations on the basic designs. Clockwise from top left: a traditional, holed nest box, painted with a water-based paint; a woodpecker box, deep to deter predators and mimic the inside of a tree trunk; a swift nesting box under house eaves; an open-fronted box on an ivy-covered fence.

MAKE YOUR OWN THRUSH BASKET

Song thrushes and blackbirds are adaptable when nesting. You can make a simple bowl-shaped structure for them to nest in.

Thrushes nest in low cover, well concealed from potential predators such as magpies or hawks. Traditionally they have relied on nesting in hedges and ditches around fields, but since farmland is now more intensively worked, these habitats (and a lot of the food that thrushes eat, such as worms and other invertebrates) have been lost. Increasingly thrushes look to nest in vegetation in gardens.

You can encourage them by making a basic nest for them to move into and adapt. In the wild, thrushes build a mud bowl, then add softer material on the outside to line and camouflage their nest. The thrush basket we make here follows the same process, starting with a sieve as it is the ideal shape and has drainage holes, although a plastic colander would also work well (avoid a metal colander as it would retain too much heat). This is best made and installed in winter.

Alternatively, or in addition, mount an old shelf to a fence, wall, or outbuilding near vegetation at least 1m (3ft) high. This will provide a sheltered platform for a thrush to build her nest on – or for you to locate your home-made thrush basket.

YOU WILL NEED

- Plastic or metal sieve or plastic colander
- Scissors
- Mud
- Bradawl or screwdriver
- Tree cuttings, loose twigs, moss, or other plant material for lining the outside of the nest
- Wire or garden twine

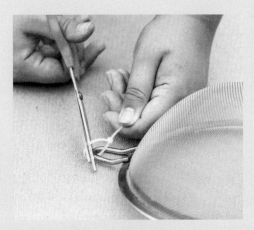

1. Remove loose items

Remove any hanging items from your sieve, such as mesh that could break, tags, or any hoops that birds may get caught on.

2. Line the inside of the sieve

Add a layer of wet mud to the inside of the sieve, pressing it down to create the basic shape of the nesting bowl.

3. Add nesting materials

Weave some nesting materials into the outside of the sieve. If necessary, use a bradawl or screwdriver to enlarge the holes. Here we're weaving some conifer stems through the holes.

4. Position your "nest"

Once your sieve is covered with natural nesting materials, find a suitable location in your garden. Choose a place with plenty of cover, such as on a thick branch near the trunk of a tree. Wedge the nest into place securely. Then fix it to the tree with wire or garden twine, ensuring that no sharp ends are sticking out.

Black eyestripe

BLUE TIT
Cyanistes caeruleus

Size Length: 10–12cm (4–4¾in); wingspan: 17–21cm (6¾–8¼in).

ID features Yellow, green, and blue with white face and small black bib. Colouring of the male is brighter than the female, especially in the blue on the head; juveniles have less coloration. Long claws allow it to be acrobatic; short beak enables it to feed from plants and small crevices. Very vocal, fast alarm call. Song consists of sharp notes followed by a trill at a lower pitch.

Habitat Mainly woodlands, hedgerows, parks, and gardens. Resident and widespread in Europe.

Feeding Insects, especially caterpillars, but also aphids and leaf miner grubs. Often gleans food from window frames. Readily uses tube feeders full of seed mix or peanuts, suet blocks, and suet balls, but will also take from ground feeders.

Plants Very active feeding on a variety of plants, hunting for insects and seeds.

Breeding Forms a nest from moss, fur, and grass felted together with feathers or soft fur. Sometimes takes to small-holed nest boxes, although will nest in any box or object converted to a nest box (such as an old boot). Can be territorial with other species such as great tits and house sparrows. Breeding season April to June. Produces 1 or 2 broods of 5 to 16 eggs, incubating for 12 to 16 days. Typical lifespan is 2 to 3 years, although some have been recorded up to 9 years old.

GREAT TIT
Parus major

Size Length: 13–15cm (5–6in); wingspan: 23–25cm (9–10in).

ID features Green above, yellow below, with large white cheeks in black head, and black stripe down breast. Male has a broader chest stripe; juvenile is often paler version of the adult. Rounded body; bigger and bolder than the blue tit. Long claws enable it to be agile on trees and feeders; short beak allows it to eat insects and spiders from trees. Distinctive "teacher, teacher, teacher" song from late winter through to early summer, and a "chink, chink" call.

Habitat Woodlands, hedgerows, parks, and gardens. Resident and common across Europe. Rarely move far from where they hatched. Mostly non-migratory.

Feeding Flying insects such as moths; also spiders. Eats berries and seeds in winter when insects are scarce. Readily feeds from tube feeders, suet feeders, and ground feeders. Can show aggression at bird feeders.

Plants Beech mast and other seeds in winter.

Breeding Nests in woodlands, parks, and gardens, including those with limited vegetation. Uses moss and grasses. Takes to large-holed nest boxes, although territorial and needs space between tit boxes. Starts to defend breeding territory in January. Breeds from April to June, producing 1 or 2 broods of up to 12 eggs per brood. Incubation is 15 days. Typical lifespan is 3 to 4 years, but some have been recorded up to 10 years.

White cheek

LONG-TAILED TIT
Aegithalos caudatus

Size Length: 13–15cm (5–6in); wingspan: 16–19cm (6¼–7½in).

ID features A ball-and-stick shape with a round pink, black, and white body, and slender tail longer than the body. Juveniles are white with a red eye ring. Long claws make it agile; short beak is ideal for picking out insects. Often heard calling to one another in roaming flocks.

Habitat Woods, hedgerows, farmland, parks, gardens with dense undergrowth. Resident in most of Europe.

Feeding Mainly on spiders, insects, and their larvae, but also berry trees. Will use garden feeders; particularly likes peanuts, suet blocks, and suet balls. Often roams in large flocks and family groups, and these can displace other birds from feeders.

Plants Thorny bushes for nesting; feeds on insects in trees such as oak, ash, and sycamore.

Breeding Nests are large balls of moss typically in forks in branches, held together and attached with spider's web then camouflaged with birch bark and lichen. Breeding starts in early April. Produces 1 or 2 broods of 5 to 16 eggs, incubating for 14 days. Roosts in groups at night to stay warm. Typical lifespan is 2 to 3 years.

COAL TIT
Periparus ater

Size Length: 10–12cm (4–4¾in); wingspan: 17–21cm (6¾–8¼in).

ID features A tiny, rounded, dull-coloured tit with distinctive white cheeks, large black bib, and white patch on back of neck. Short, slender beak and long claws are perfectly adapted for feeding in trees, especially conifers. Often heard singing from perches giving a "sithcu-sitchu-sitchu" call similar to that of the great tit but softer and higher pitched.

Habitat Woodlands, especially conifer woods, hedgerows, parks, and gardens. Resident in most parts of Europe; some birds migrate to UK from continental Europe in winter.

Feeding Insects and seeds, hoarding food in tree crevices. Readily uses tube feeders, suet blocks, and suet balls, but will also take from ground feeders. Loves sunflower seeds. Can be timid among larger species and prefers a quieter feeder.

Plants Conifers and beech are a source for insects and seeds. Uses plant materials in its nesting.

Breeding Breeding season from April to June. Nests in holes in trees, making its nest from moss, fur, and grass felted together with feathers or soft fur. May take to small-holed nest boxes easily although can be bullied by larger species. Produces 1 or 2 broods of 7 to 12 eggs, incubating for about 15 days. Can form flocks with other tits in winter. Typical lifespan is around 2 or 3 years.

Black, pink, and white back

FINCH HEALTH

Finches are prone to disease spread by shared contact with infected surfaces. To prevent spread of disease, clean garden feeders regularly.

GOLDFINCH
Carduelis carduelis

Size Length: 12–13cm (4¾–5in); wingspan: 21–26cm (8¼–10in).

ID features Pale brown with red, black, and white face; black wing with broad yellow band; juvenile is buff with streaks on the back, breast, and head. Triangular beak. Call has buzzing noises with tri-syllables.

Habitat Found in scrubland, parks, gardens, and woods containing birch. Resident in most of Europe.

Feeding Looks for seeds in grasslands and on trees. Eats mixes from tube feeders, especially niger seeds.

Plants Grasses, teasels, and thistles for their seeds. Uses plants in its nesting but also for feeding and foraging.

Breeding Nests high in trees, often near others. Female creates nest in a neat, rounded shape, lined with soft materials such as thistle, animal fur, and mosses, attached to the branch with spider's silk. Breeding season begins in April. Two broods a year, each of 3 to 7 eggs with incubation of 10 to 14 days. Typical lifespan between 2 and 3 years.

GREENFINCH
Chloris chloris

Size Length: 14–16cm (5½–6¼in); wingspan: 21–26cm (8¼–10in).

ID features Green, with pinkish beak and yellow streaks on wing and tail; juvenile is similar to adult but has a streaky appearance on the head and back. Triangular beak. Song often varies with the most common a buzzing noise, or a trilling melody.

Habitat Found in woodland edges, parks, and gardens. Resident throughout most of Europe.

Feeding Areas with open spaces for feeding where seed-bearing plants are found. Common garden visitors, eating mixes from tube feeders and bird tables; will often feed off the discarded seed on the ground.

Plants Seeds and berries for food. Uses dense shrubs for nesting.

Breeding Nests in dense vegetation such as conifers or thick hedges. Has an open nest constructed from twigs and lined with mosses and animal fur. Breeding season from March to July, with pairs having 2 or 3 broods per season. Nests have 4 to 6 eggs which are incubated for 13 to 14 days. Lifespan typically around 2 years although many fall victim to garden diseases before then.

Yellow wing band

130/131 BIRDS / FINCH FAMILY

CHAFFINCH
Fringilla coelebs

Size Length: 14–16cm (5½–6¼in); wingspan: 24–29cm (9½–11½in).

ID features Male has a pinkish-orange breast and grey head; female has a brown head and nape with grey around the face. Both have black wings with a white wing bar. Stout, strong beak. Song is very powerful and one of the most recognizable songs, consisting of a descending cadence with trills. Frequently makes a "huuitt" noise.

Habitat Found in woodlands, parks, and gardens. Breeds throughout most of Europe.

Feeding Primarily on lawns looking for insects and seed; very common in gardens and on garden feeders. Will eat mixes from tube feeders, bird tables, ground feeders, and wall feeders.

Plants Forages in trees for seeds and berries.

Breeding Nests in park and garden hedges; it is an open nester, meaning it will not take to a nest box. Nests are typically created out of twigs and moss, lined with further moss, fur, or feathers. Breeding season is April through to August, with 1 brood of 4 or 5 eggs, incubation 11 to 13 days. Typical lifespan between 3 and 4 years, although many fall victim to garden diseases before then.

Male

Red breast

Male

BULLFINCH
Pyrrhula pyrrhula

Size Length: 14–17cm (5½–6¾in); wingspan: 22–26cm (8½–10in).

ID features Male has bright red cheeks, breast, and belly with a grey back and glossy back cap. Female has a glossy black cap, grey around the cheeks, brown back, and a rust-coloured breast and belly. Easily identifiable in flight with glossy black wings and tail and a white rump patch. Call is a short but melodic whistle. Song is similar with melodic whistles and finishing in a descending tone.

Habitat Primarily woodlands, parks, and gardens. Resident in most parts of Europe.

Feeding Feeds in dense scrub and thick hedges, from trees, foraging for seeds and fruits.

Plants Eats fruit buds in spring, and berries from elder and bramble.

Breeding Nests in hedges and bushes, or in small trees with dense vegetation. Often creates nest from twigs and small sticks, lining it with animal fur, moss, and lichen. Breeding season is March to June, with 1 brood of 4 or 5 eggs, incubating for 14 to 21 days. Typical lifespan is around 2 years.

SISKIN
Carduelis spinus

Size Length: 11–12cm (4¼–4¾in); wingspan: 20–23cm (8–9in).

ID features Male is bright yellow on the head and breast and has a black cap on the head; female has an olive-coloured back and head with streaks. Song is a mixture of twittering and trilling noises with some mimicry.

Habitat Found throughout woodlands, parks, and gardens, particularly in areas with conifer and spruce. Breeds in northern or upland parts of Europe.

Feeding Feeds in open woodland with birch, along rivers with alder, and in conifer plantations. Common garden visitor, eating mixes from tube feeders, and will feed off the discarded seed on the ground.

Plants Conifer, birch, and alder for seeds. Uses trees for nesting.

Breeding Nests in conifers, including pine, and other woodlands, often nesting near to one another. Open nests constructed out of twigs and lined with mosses and animal fur. Breeding season in March to July; pairs often have 1 or 2 broods per year, each of 4 to 6 eggs, incubating in 11 to 14 days. Typical lifespan is between 3 and 4 years.

EUROPEAN ROBIN
Erithacus rubecula

Size Length: 12–14cm (4¾–5½in); wingspan: 20–22cm (8–8½in).

ID features Adults have red breasts, while juveniles are brown with speckles. Short, slender beak. Flat feet ideal for foraging for worms, while long claws are often used for perching on trees for singing. Contact call is a ticking noise. Song is very soft, common to hear around dawn and dusk. Almost uniquely, robins sing all year as they keep their territories through the winter.

Habitat Found within areas of vegetation that include a perch to sing from. Abundant in gardens, particularly where there is natural shelter. Resident across Europe with some spring and autumn migration between northeast and southwest.

Feeding Often looks for worms and snails on the ground. Also takes to bird feeders for mealworms and suet, particularly bird tables and ground feeders, although will use tube feeders with a dish base.

Plants Uses sheltering plants such as ivy, bramble, and holly, as well as trees and shrubs to nest in.

Breeding Naturally breeds in woodlands, gardens, parks, and anywhere with dense vegetation. Takes readily to gardens, making a nest in anything available – even old boots and plant pots. Will also use open-fronted nest boxes and roosting pockets. Breeding season begins around April with 3 or 4 broods of 6 to 8 eggs; incubation is 12 to 14 days. Typical lifespan between 1 and 3 years.

Dark spots on
pale breast ....

SONG THRUSH
Turdus philomelos

Size Length: 22–24cm (8½–9½in); wingspan:
33–36cm (13–14in).

ID features Brown above, yellow-buff below, with
V-shaped blackish spots, mostly on the breast and
flank. Long, stout beak. Flat feet ideal for hopping
around the ground foraging. Notable song, varied
and loud, repeating each phrase 3 or 4 times, often
mimicking other noises nearby.

Habitat Often seen around hedgerows, parks, and
gardens, and in deciduous woods. Breeds in most
parts of Europe; many move southwest for the winter.

Feeding Worms and larvae in the ground; in the
winter feeds on berries and fruit. Feeds on slugs and
snails, smashing snail shells on a rock to expose the
body. Visits gardens to feed on discarded seed,
although prefers to stay near to vegetation, often
looking for discarded fruit from trees.

Plants Will feed upon the fruit of hawthorn, yew, ivy,
rowan, cherry, and apple in winter.

Breeding Nests in ivy and shrubs, using moss and
twigs in its nest, sometimes with berries. Breeding
season begins in March; 2 or 3 broods, each of 4 or 5
per year; incubation is 14 to 15 days. Typical lifespan
between 3 and 4 years.

BLACKBIRD
Turdus merula

Size Length: 23–25cm (9–10in); wingspan: 34–38cm
(13–15in).

ID features Male is black with yellow beak and yellow
eye ring; female is brown all over; juvenile is brown with
streaks all over. Stout beak. Sings and calls frequently
and has one of the most recognizable songs heard
from perches at dawn and throughout the breeding
season. Often makes a clucking sound when alarmed.

Habitat Anywhere food is available, in parks, gardens,
and woodlands. Commonly seen in urban areas.
Breeds throughout Europe.

Feeding Worms, larvae, and insects in the soil, and
very commonly seen on berry trees and foraging for
apples. Will use garden feeders such as bird tables and
ground feeders, and will attempt to use tube feeders
with platforms.

Plants Commonly uses rowan, hawthorn, and apple
trees in the winter.

Breeding Nests in shrubs and trees in gardens, and
will nest in eaves and platforms in outside structures
such as sheds. Breeding season is March until July.
Pairs have 2 or 3 broods per year with 4 to 6 eggs per
brood; incubation takes 13 to 14 days. Typical lifespan
is 3 to 5 years, although can live up to 10 years.

Yellow eye ring ....

Male

Grey cap

Male

HOUSE SPARROW
Passer domesticus

Size Length: 14–15cm (5½–6in); wingspan: 21–26cm (8¼–10in).

ID features Male has brown back, black bib, and a grey cap; female is brown all over with a buff breast; juvenile is similar to female with a streaked breast. Short, triangular beak, ideal for eating seeds.

Habitat Found in open land, parks, and gardens; often seen in urban areas. Resident throughout Europe although populations are declining.

Feeding Feeds on lawns looking for insects, and commonly on garden feeders. Will eat seeds from tube feeders but also from bird tables, ground feeders, and wall feeders.

Plants Uses plant materials in its nest. Needs dense bushes as cover.

Breeding Nests in communal groups, often in parks and garden hedges as well as house eaves and outdoor buildings, and will use a nest box placed near to an entrance to the eaves. Breeding from April through to August; typically has 2 or 3 broods, depending on food availability, of 4 to 7 eggs, with incubation of 12 to 13 days. Typical lifespan is 3 to 4 years.

WOOD PIGEON
Columba palumbus

Size Length: 38–43cm (15–17in); wingspan: 68–77cm (27–30in).

ID features A big, grey pigeon with white on the neck and broad white band on each wing. Tail has a pale central band and dark tip. Short beak. Short legs with flat feet, waddling walk. Monotone call with simple "hooh-hrooo". Noisy wing claps on take off.

Habitat Open grasslands including garden lawns; often breeds nearby in woodlands, parks, and tree-lined gardens. Will sometimes breed in outdoor structures like barns or sheds. Breeds in many areas of Europe.

Feeding Ground feeder, often seen under bird feeders looking for dropped food, although will land on open-topped bird tables. Not picky with its food, often eating anything including shoots, buds, grain, old vegetable matter.

Plants Pecks at leaves of clovers and beans. Uses deciduous trees to create its twig nest.

Breeding Breeds throughout the year, typically from May to October, but has been known to begin breeding as early as February with multiple broods. Each brood consists of 2 or 3 eggs, hatching after 17 to 19 days. Typical lifespan is between 3 and 4 years, although some have been recorded up to 17 years.

Black collar ....

COLLARED DOVE
Streptopelia decaocto

Size Length: 29–33cm (11½–13in); wingspan: 48–53cm (19–21in).

ID features Slim dove, mostly pale buff, with a black "collar"; underside of tail black and white. Short, slender beak. Monotone call with classic "doo-dooo-doo" call; often very talkative when performing courtships.

Habitat Open grasslands including garden lawns. Breeds in many areas of Europe.

Feeding Ground feeder, often seen under bird feeders looking for dropped food, although will land on open-topped bird tables.

Plants Feeds on hawthorn and other berry trees. Uses deciduous trees for nesting.

Breeding Nests in woodlands, parks, and tree-lined gardens near to where it feeds. Will also breed in outdoor structures such as barns or sheds, sometimes in strange places such as satellite dishes. Has multiple broods of 2 eggs, incubation around 18 days; some birds begin creating a new nest before previous young have fledged. Typical lifespan is between 3 and 4 years, although has been recorded up to 15 years.

JACKDAW
Corvus monedula

Size Length: 30–34cm (12–13in); wingspan: 64–73cm (25–29in).

ID features Small, grey-black crow with a grey neck and black cap. Long, stout beak used for digging. Juveniles have a "scruffy" appearance compared with the sleeker adults. Very vocal, often heard making a "cack" noise, and chattering to one another in flight before roosting. Sometimes makes spectacular communal roosts in favoured woods.

Habitat Found in woodlands, parks, and gardens; very common in urban areas. Resident in Europe.

Feeding Primarily on insects, eggs, and worms in the soil but will also eat fruit, seeds, and scraps. Visits garden bird feeders in small groups, feeds on bird tables, at ground feeders, and will attempt to use tube feeders; takes a range of food.

Plants Forages for fruit.

Breeding Nests in woodlands, parks and gardens, often in chimneys, on buildings, and in natural areas such as rock crevices and holes in trees. Uses plant materials in its nest. Will use owl boxes. Breeding season from April to July, 1 brood per year with incubation around 20–22 days. Typical lifespan between 5 and 7 years.

MAMMALS

MAMMALS

Ranging from large badgers and foxes to tiny, shy voles and mice – as well as fast-moving bats – mammals are a large and varied group. They visit most gardens but may be hard to spot. A garden in a more rural setting is likely to see a wider range of mammals, but there are plenty to be seen in urban gardens too. Since many mammals spend their time avoiding predators, providing a safe environment in a wild garden is a good starting point for attracting and supporting more mammals.

Brown hares live among and like to eat grass. They may visit gardens in rural areas.

WHERE TO
FIND MAMMALS

It's surprisingly hard to spot mammals in the garden. Some are small, and most are practised at avoiding being seen so that they can keep safe from predators.

Many of the mammals that are likely to be seen in the garden are nocturnal, active from dusk to dawn as this is when there are fewer predators (though owls are formidable mammal hunters).

Tiny mice, voles, and shrews tend to have long noses and whiskers for sensing and smelling danger, large eyes with large pupils giving them the best sight in the dark, and large ears, which pick up all sorts of sounds. Depending on where you live, larger mammals, including weasels, stoats, hedgehogs, squirrels, moles, and rabbits also visit gardens. Rabbits, hares, badgers, and moles tend to be more prevalent in rural areas, and foxes, squirrels, and hedgehogs in towns. Bats fly over gardens in many locations (see pp.142–43). If you go out at night looking for mammals, avoid rustling and other loud noises, and bright lights darting around. It's often easier to see traces, such as footprints, a burrow or remains of food, rather than the animal itself (see pp.156–157).

Mammals in winter

Winter is a challenging time as food is scarce and it takes a lot of energy to keep warm. Hedgehogs and bats go into a dormant state of hibernation for several months during which their body temperature, and heart and breathing rates drop. Shrews, badgers, and pine martens become less active to save energy. Otters, foxes, and others increase their hunting to get them through; foxes grow a thicker coat, while otters hunt near running water that doesn't freeze.

Common shrew

Red squirrel

Stoat

Rabbit

Mole

In trees

Squirrels are acrobatic climbers and they eat, breed, and nest in trees. Pine martens are also agile climbers in their preferred habitat of coniferous trees. Smaller mammals, such as some mice and voles, will scamper up trunks and along branches to forage for nuts and seeds.

Among stones and rocks

Stone walls are a vital habitat for stoats and weasels. With their long, slim bodies, they are suited to squeezing into small gaps. You may also see them moving their young around and trying to carry prey into their dens.

In vegetation

By leaving areas of vegetation relatively undisturbed, you're likely to attract a number of small mammals, particularly voles, shrews, and rabbits. All stealthily move between plants looking for food and safety. Hedgehogs move and forage in areas of longer vegetation and among piles of leaves.

Under the ground

Look out for holes in and around your garden, near the base of trees, shrubs, or hedges. These are likely to be entrances to burrows. A small hole, around 4cm (1½in) across, indicates house mice; at the larger end, a 12cm (4½in) hole suggests rabbits. Moles create tunnel networks underground leaving mole hills of earth on the surface.

Higher altitudes

Noctules tend to fly high, normally over the tops of trees, chasing down flying beetles and moths with long, heavy wing beats. Whiskered bats also flutter among the tree canopy catching high-flying insects.

Whiskered bat

Mid-level

Small species tend to fly below the tree canopy but above hedges, as this is where they feel safest; the main predators are owls and cats. Pipistrelles such as common, soprano, and Nathusius' flit around the middle ground, often in a fast, jerky style.

Soprano
pipistrelle

Low to the ground

Bats such as lesser horseshoe, brown long-eared, and greater horseshoe are often seen "hawking" (chasing their prey) close to the ground. They focus on insects that are about to settle down for the night or moths just emerging for their night flights.

Brown
long-eared bat

Noctule

Common
pipistrelle

Lesser
horseshoe bat

WHERE BATS FLY

The only flying mammals, bats are highly intelligent, with an incredible memory for locations. They can be seen flying over gardens at dawn and dusk.

Contrary to popular belief, bats are not blind. The truth is they have little need to use their eyes. Being creatures that emerge and hunt during the dim twilight hours, bats have evolved instead to navigate via echolocation, which involves emitting a sound wave that bounces off objects, returning an echo. This echo provides vital information such as the distance and size of object that it bounces off. Bats use this knowledge to navigate in the dark, and to hunt for their prey. Bat calls are usually at a higher frequency than human ears can hear. If you use a bat detector, which processes the sounds bats make, it's possible to identify which bats are flying nearby by the sound frequency of their call (see pp.166–69).

In the daytime, bats roost in various spaces, often in large numbers. They have winter and summer roosts, in places such as in tree holes, buildings, caves, or under bridges. Female bats gather in spring in maternity roosts to give birth to and rear their pups. At dusk, bats emerge from their roost and head out to hunt. For different bat species, there are different hunting heights and methods. They use walls, houses, fences, and hedges to navigate around gardens in search of their main source of food: insects, which are often found near flowers and over water.

WHAT MAMMALS EAT

Food is relatively easy to come by for smaller mammals. Larger mammals roam further to find enough food, and may visit gardens to feed.

Mice, voles, and shrews are like a garden clean-up crew. They hunt and eat a variety of insects and invertebrates such as snails, slugs, and woodlice, and they also eat vegetation such as bulbs, grasses, and seed pods. As with most types of wildlife, plants are the key to attracting them. Many mammals eat plants, but they are equally important to attract insects and invertebrates which are an important part of the diet of many mammals.

Low-growing plants

Stems, flowers, leaves, and bulbs may all be nibbled by mammals. Rabbits and hares, especially, may be disliked by gardeners if they feast on prized ornamental grasses, flowers, and edibles (see box, opposite).

Nuts and berries

Grey and red squirrels, along with other small mammals such as mice and voles, look for chestnut, hazel, and oak trees where the nuts drop for them to gather and stash for the winter in the ground or in their dreys. Berries and fruit are also eaten by mice and voles, and occasionally foxes.

LIVING WITH HUNGRY MAMMALS

Mammals are resourceful, and if they are hungry and visit our gardens, they will take opportunities to grab easy food. Foxes, for example, look in places where they know our scraps will be; many areas now use wheelie bins to protect household waste from hungry mammals. If rabbits are eating your vegetables or other plants, consider using chicken wire to surround a bed to about 1m (3ft), or make a wire cage around a particular plant.

Soil and soil invertebrates

Small mammals and hedgehogs search for slugs and snails to eat. Badgers and moles have earthworms as an important food source, so healthy soil will benefit these predators.

Other mammals and birds

Weasels and pine martens hunt for mice and voles, often raiding their burrows. Stoats are also fierce predators, taking rabbits as well as mice and voles. Pine martens will take birds. Foxes will eat pigeons and rats as well as animals that they find that are already dead.

Water creatures

Ponds can occasionally provide fish and amphibians for otters to eat. The insects that are attracted to water provide a steady food source for bats such as Daubenton's bats, known as "water bats", which can be seen dancing over the water surface looking for egg-laying insects such as stonefly, damselfly, and midges.

PROVIDING FOOD AND WATER FOR MAMMALS

It's possible to supplement the natural sources of food and water, either on an area of grass or in purpose-made feeders.

Autumn is a good time to put food out for mammals as they are stocking up on nutrition before the scarcity of the winter months. Squirrels cache their food and store it ready for when they emerge in the spring, while others will appreciate a regular, accessible supply. If you are feeding mammals using bowls or other feeders, keep them clean by washing them daily outside with hot, soapy water to reduce the possible spread of disease.

Nut mixes
Adding squirrel feeders or ground feeders to the garden allows us to provide food similar to that which squirrels will find in the wild. Peanut feeders (like those for birds) or bowls of mixed peanuts, walnuts, and even mealworms are great sources of fibre and protein.

Eggs
Boiled eggs are full of protein and are eaten by mammals, including foxes and pine martens. Adding a few whole eggs to your garden feeding area or in a dish will allow foxes and martens to come in and carry them off to eat elsewhere or for their young.

Hedgehog food

There are specific mixes designed with hedgehogs in mind. These are either wet mixes or dry biscuits (above), which you can add to bowls in a box with an entrance cut in one side for small mammals and hedgehogs to get to the food. You can give hedgehogs and other mammals meat-based cat or dog food, although it's best to use specialist mixes and semi-natural ingredients such as nuts. Never give milk to hedgehogs; they are lactose intolerant and drinking milk can lead to health issues. For more on how to care for hedgehogs in your garden, see pp.154–55.

Peanut butter

Badgers love peanuts. You can put peanuts on your lawn or on a patch of soil near to a wooded area, or smear some peanut butter (above) on tree branches or logs to attract in badgers; birds, mice, and even pine martens may also feed on peanut butter.

WATER SOURCES

A water dish such as a cat's bowl is a simple way to provide water for garden mammals. Ponds can also provide a reliable water source. Larger mammals, such as badgers and foxes, as well as small ones, will come to drink. It's important to consider access for small mammals, as they may fall in to deeper water and not be able to climb out. Add stones or other platforms in deep water for small mammals to climb onto. In a pond, ensure there are access points with sloping rocks or ladders for small mammals who may need help to climb out.

SAFE SPACES FOR MAMMALS

Mammals need shelter, in particular during the breeding season and in order to hibernate. Small mammals that are frequently preyed upon also need safe refuges all year.

When breeding, sleeping, and hibernating (see p.140), mammals are at their most vulnerable. They look for a safe space that offers entry points under cover where they won't be ambushed by predators (see opposite). They also need warmth and access to food and water nearby. They may make underground burrows, or nests in trees or under shrubs and hedges.

Breeding

In a garden, mammals will look to create a nest or burrow that is secure enough to safely raise young without any predators being able to detect pregnant females or new mothers and their youngsters. The smaller species tend to have more offspring to ensure some survive to adulthood, whereas larger species have fewer in a litter but will remain with them to adulthood to give them the best chance of survival. Otters, for example, have one or two litters of three or four pups each year, whereas mice can have two or three litters a year of six to ten pups. Bats gather in maternity roosts to raise their pups all together (see p.143).

If you think that a species may be nesting in your garden, watch for more activity as the adults may be looking for food for their young; never disturb active nesting chambers. As the young mammals emerge and start to learn to move around the garden, you may see them. Shrews make a shrew-chain with mum leading the young around vegetation and cover. Foxes can also be seen in gardens from March to July when they are feeding their cubs.

Otters make a nest known as a "holt" in a riverbank among tree roots with cover from plants. The mother otter raises her cubs in the holt, taking them out gradually to learn to swim and hunt.

Hedges

Laurel, spindle, holly, and wild privet are all fantastic plants for hedges as garden boundaries instead of walls and fences. They form dense barriers, with plenty of shelter, but still allow wildlife such as foxes, badgers, and hedgehogs access into your garden. In addition, laurel and holly are evergreen, and so form a year-round screen. Hedges offer soil for rabbits and other small mammals to dig out their underground burrows in a sheltered spot.

Compost heaps

Mammals thrive in semi-natural spaces such as compost heaps. These heaps degrade over time, and are full of oxygen, meaning other smaller creatures such as worms, slugs, and snails use them for feeding on decaying plants. They are therefore prime hunting grounds for hedgehogs, mice, voles, and shrews, which may shelter nearby if there is cover. Hedgehogs love to use compost heaps as a hibernation location as they are often undisturbed, warm, and provide them with enough cover that predators will not find them.

Trees

Grey squirrels create their nests, known as "dreys", in treetops, while red squirrels find disused holes or crevices in tree trunks as a nesting location in which they can raise their young. Pine martens also look for hollows in trees to breed. The base of mature trees provides a great habitat for foxes, badgers, stoats, weasels, and mice to dig and create burrows and dens as the soil is much looser around the tree roots.

NEST BOXES
FOR MAMMALS

Specialist nest boxes and homes for different
mammals can provide a safe space in the garden
at ground level or on walls or tree trunks.

A variety of mammals need help, especially declining species such as bats, which have lost roosting habitats as old buildings have been repaired or replaced (see pp.152–153 for bat boxes). It's possible to provide a safe space for mammals, and many species take to them fairly easily. Your aim is to provide a shelter that offers similar conditions to a burrow or a hollow tree – wherever the species would naturally go. These boxes will be used for different purposes: some mice use them to rest in during the day, while red squirrels use a box to breed and raise young.

Hedgehog house

Houses of various designs offer a safe space for hedgehogs to hibernate and rest during the day. Some designs have an entrance straight into the nesting chamber, while others have an entrance chamber separate from the nesting chamber, offering more protection from predators. For more ideas on making your garden a haven for hedgehogs, see pp.154–55.

Mouse box

This box has a wire frame with woven stems around the outside, and a waterproof layer inside at the top. With the entrance hole next to the trunk of a tree, it attracts mice and voles, which can scuttle in safely from the trunk (or it may be used by birds such as wrens and treecreepers). You can add soft material inside such as straw and sawdust to encourage small mammals to hibernate over the winter and sleep during the day – occasionally you'll see more than one creature inside the box. The box is attached to a tree at a height of 1.5–2m (5–6½ft).

Red squirrel box

A red squirrel box replicates the natural conditions of a tree cavity. It is long, rectangular, and dark inside, with grooves inside and out to enable the squirrels to enter and exit. The entrance hole is 8cm (3in) in diameter. Squirrels may return to the same box year after year and will use it during the breeding season.

BAT BOXES

Help reverse the decline in bat populations
by providing additional places for them
to roost and breed.

We usually see bats in the garden between March and October when insects are abundant. Females gather in a maternity roost in spring where they produce and rear one pup per year. In late autumn, bats move to a separate location to roost for hibernation.

Bat boxes provide roosts for different colonies of bats. The entrance size and design of the box determine which bats can use it; greater and lesser horseshoe bats hang upside down to roost, but most other species prefer to roost in crevices. They often have a "ladder": a series of horizontal grooves that the bat can cling on to as it enters the box. Some bats are much more likely to take to a box (see pp.166–69), and it's worth checking which species are found in your area before choosing a box or rack.

An open, draught-free spot is ideal for a bat box, with an unobstructed flight path, and preferably with direct sunlight for much of the day. Some can be integrated into the design of your house, near the eaves of your roof, or even 2–3m (6½–10ft) up a tree. Once the box is up, leave it alone for the bats to find and use. You can tell if it's occupied by looking for droppings underneath, and by observing it at dusk to see if there are any bats leaving. It's illegal to disturb a roost (see p.167), so you must only observe it once it's in use. Because waste will fall out of the bottom of the box, it does not need cleaning.

Wooden bat box

This is a simple rectangular box suitable for a variety of bats, including pipistrelles. Bats fly upwards to the entrance, which usually has grooved slats that bats use to crawl into the box. With a little carpentry knowledge, it's possible to make your own box; the RSPB website offers simple instructions. This type of bat box needs to be fixed 2.5–5m (8–16ft) off the ground on a mature tree or the wall of a building.

Woodcrete bat box

A mix of wood and concrete is used for these boxes, and offers good insulation, as well as being very hardwearing. Various designs are available. This type of box can be fixed to a building and it will be used by pipistrelle species.

Bat brick

Bat bricks are a relatively new addition to the bat box market but are an ingenious idea. These

bricks are integrated as part of the structure when building a house, an outdoor shed, or an extension. There are two types of bat brick: one allows bats to access a cavity inside the house, the other has a roosting chamber attached to the brick. Crevice-nesting bats such as pipistrelles take to bat bricks.

Clockwise from top left: a woodcrete bat box with a small slat at the front for entry, and removable dividers to create smaller crevices within the box or one big space; a wooden bat box with an entrance gap underneath; a bat brick the size of a breeze block with the entrance underneath.

Bat rack

Whilst many species like to cling on to surfaces such as stone, beams, and wood, some, such as greater and lesser horseshoe bats, hang upside-down using their strong feet. A bat rack offers a safe space inside the roofs of stone buildings, sheds, or even the roof space of your house. These spaces are ones that the bats may already use, but the rack provides a purpose-made roost.

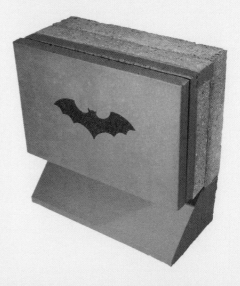

MAKE A
HEDGEHOG HAVEN

Hedgehogs have simple needs: food, water, shelter, and the ability to travel to find these things. You can add these elements to your garden to make it more enticing for hedgehogs.

Small but full of character, hedgehogs used to be a common visitor to gardens, but in recent years they have declined in numbers. Hedgehogs can walk up to 2km (just over a mile) per night, seeking increasingly scarce opportunities to feed, hibernate, and breed. As they prefer to use level ground, many are killed crossing roads, while the loss of hedges and other dense vegetation has taken away the cover they need. A hedgehog may also try to visit multiple gardens to find everything they're looking for, but if access is blocked by fencing, they can't move around. In the garden, they also face hazards such as poisoning from insecticides and slug pellets (see p.41), and injuries from garden forks, strimming cords, lawnmowers, and plant support wires.

Making small adaptations to your garden can give hedgehogs a safe space, and once they start using your garden, they will continue to visit, and even bring their young.

1. Provide access

Cut a hole in your fence to allow hedgehogs to pass in and out of your garden safely, and to dart out if they feel uneasy or are startled. A good size for a hole (which can be square or arched) is 13 x 13cm (5 x 5in) as this lets them pass through, but is too small for most pets. You can cut a fence before you erect it, or make the hole when it's in situ. If you have a brick wall, see if it's possible to remove a couple of bricks at ground level. Once you have created your hole, ensure it remains clear.

2. Plant up a wild border

Provide dense planting with grasses and shrubs so that hedgehogs can forage for food and move undetected. Include deciduous plants so they can use the fallen leaves for their nests. Check hedges, leaf piles, and compost heaps before disturbing them as hedgehogs may shelter underneath.

3. Create a watering station

Add a shallow dish to your garden for them to drink from, with pebbles inside and out to ensure there are safe entry and exit points as young ones will struggle with obstacles. Clean the dish and refill the water often.

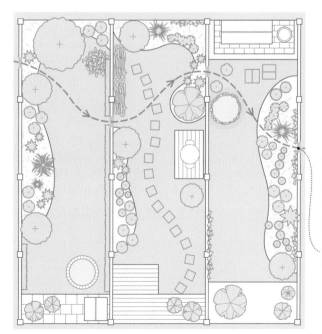

4. Make a hedgehog highway

We can't save and protect species alone. Chat to your neighbours and see whether you can create a hedgehog highway by providing access points between hedgehog-friendly gardens. By linking up multiple gardens, we can provide hedgehogs with a greater variety of food sources and shelter opportunities. If they can move between gardens, this reduces the need for them to cross roads, and creates a larger, safer space for hedgehog families.

Gap in fence for hedgehog highway

CREATE A MAMMAL TRACKER

It's often hard to spot mammals that are nocturnal or move under cover. Creating ways to track mammals will help you identify the species that visit your garden.

There are two ways of creating tracking areas in your garden: tracking mats and tracking tubes. Each works by making an impression of the footprints of creatures that walk over that area. It's then possible to identify the footprints to match them to the mammals. You can try various areas of the garden to compare how often each is visited, or routes taken by different mammals. You'll find an introduction to print identification on pages 176–77, and other guidance online, for example on the Wildlife Trusts website.

Tracking mats are filled with sand or soil, and any animal walking over the mat will leave indented footprints; they work well for larger mammals such as foxes, badgers, hedgehogs, and weasels, as well as small mammals. Tracking tubes are suitable only for smaller mammals (which will fit through the tube), such as voles, mice, shrews, and occasionally hedgehogs, weasels, and stoats. The tubes can be placed on the ground, like the tracking mats, or fastened to a branch to record small mammals in the tree canopy.

Make a tracking mat

Tracking mats are simple to set up. Find a thin baking tray or plastic tray and fill it with damp sand or soil. Ensure the sand or soil is only damp and is not wet, as smaller mammals will leave less of an imprint in wet conditions. Place the tracking mat in your garden near some vegetation and add some food to attract the mammals; leave the mat in place overnight. When mammals come to investigate, their feet will leave an imprint in the sand or soil that can be identified later on.

1. Prepare the tray
Pour some sand into the tray and smooth it with a straight edge. Spray it with water to dampen it.

2. Position the tray

Add some food to the centre of the sand, such as plain peanuts or dry cat food, and place the mat carefully under some cover (for example, beside a hedge).

Make a tracking tube

A tracking tube works in a similar way to a tracking mat, but the mammals leave footprints in ink on paper instead of imprints in sand. You can use plastic guttering, or reuse an old juice carton, removing the ends. Tape a piece of paper inside the tube. Add some ink to one end, directly onto the paper, or on a sponge or ink pad if it is likely to dry out. Place a small amount of food such as peanuts in the centre. Mammals will pass over the ink to reach the food, leaving behind footprints that you can try to identify.

3. Try to identify mammal tracks

Enticed by the food, mammals will come and go, leaving their tracks. Here the larger tracks are squirrels and the smaller ones are mice.

Positioning the tracking tube

Place the tube among vegetation or secure it to a roughly horizontal branch of a tree with cable ties, wire, or garden twine.

WOOD MOUSE
Apodemus sylvaticus

Size Body: 8–10cm (3–4in) long: tail 7–9cm (2¾–3½in).

ID features Dark brown with golden-brown flanks and pale beige underside; large ears and eyes and a longer tail compared to other species. Much browner than the house mouse. Nocturnal, often seen moving around in the night with a bounding gait.

Habitat One of the most widespread mammals in the British Isles, found in woodland, rough grassland, and very commonly in gardens, houses, and outbuildings.

Feeding Invertebrates such as worms, centipedes, and caterpillars; seeds, fruits, and berries. Will eat bird seed in gardens, and often seen on bird tables. Gathers food stores in autumn for the winter months, which it keeps in underground burrows, old birds' nests, and even in garden bird and mouse boxes.

Plants Gathers berries from tree species such as hawthorn, ivy, and blackthorn; gathers seeds from numerous plants.

Breeding Has about 4 litters per year with 4 to 8 pups in each. Can also breed over the winter if suitable food sources are available. Does not hibernate. Typical lifespan is 1 to 2 years.

YELLOW-NECKED MOUSE
Apodemus flavicollis

Size Body: 9–12cm (3½–4¾in) long; tail: 8–12cm (3–4¾in).

ID features Speckled brown fur on the head, back, and sides with a white underbelly. Has large ears, protruding eyes, and a long tail. Name is derived from the yellowish band around the front of the neck, forming a collar.

Habitat Found in southern half of England and Wales; mostly a woodland species, but found in gardens (and lofts and outhouses) that are close to woodland.

Feeding Mostly tree seeds, but also eats other plants and invertebrates – similar to wood mouse. Can often be seen around bird feeders looking for discarded seeds on the ground, although also an excellent climber.

Plants Gathers berries from hawthorn, ivy, and blackthorn. Feeds on tree seeds, mostly from beech, sycamore, hazel, and oak.

Breeding Female has 3 or 4 pregnancies from February to October with litters of 2 to 11 pups. Does not hibernate. Typical lifespan is 1 to 2 years.

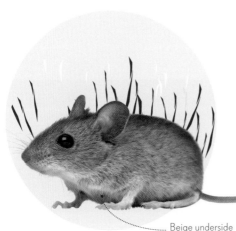

.... Beige underside

HOUSE MOUSE
Mus musculus

Size Body: 6–10cm (2½–4in) long; tail: around 6–10cm (2½–4in).

ID features Grey-brown with rounded ears and a pointed nose; the tail is often scaly. Lacks the white colouring under the belly and the chin of other species, and often has a more rat-like appearance, though much smaller.

Habitat One of the most widespread mammal species, primarily found around farm buildings, warehouses, sheds, and garages although not often seen in homes any longer. Common in gardens, including those that are all paved.

Feeding Seeds and nuts; will often take discarded food, especially around farm buildings and sheds. Also eats insects and spiders outdoors. Gathers food stores for winter in underground burrows, old birds' nests, and even in garden bird and mouse boxes.

Plants Not often reliant upon plants but does look for grains, fruits, and seeds. Will feed upon crops such as barley and maize, on flowers with seeds such as sunflowers, and trees with fruits such as hawthorn.

Breeding Can have up to 10 litters a year with 6 to 8 pups. Can also breed over the winter if suitable food sources are available. Does not hibernate. Typical lifespan is 1 to 2 years.

HARVEST MOUSE
Micromys minutus

Size Body: 5–7cm (2–2¾in) long; tail: around 6cm (2½in) long.

ID features Very small species, golden-brown with a white underbelly. Tail is prehensile, acting as a fifth limb to grasp tree and plant stems.

Habitat Lives in long grassland, reedbeds, hedgerows, farmland, and occasionally around woodland edges. Builds a spherical nest of tightly woven grass, high up in tall reeds and grasses.

Feeding Focuses on seeds and fruits, but will occasionally eat invertebrates such as aphids and woodlice. Also eats grains from cereal heads such as barley and maize, leaving sickle-shaped remains.

Plants Seeds and fruits found in grassland areas, such as willow and hawthorn; seed heads in reedbeds such as those of tussock grasses.

Breeding Female gives birth between May and October, producing up to 3 litters a year with each litter having 3 to 8 pups. Does not hibernate. Typical lifespan is 1 to 2 years.

Small ears ....

BANK VOLE
Myodes glareolus

Size Body: 8–12cm (3–4¾in) long; tail: 4–6cm (1½–2in).

ID features Chestnut-brown around the head, back, and sides with white belly. Much richer in colour than field voles, and has a much longer tail. Voles have a blunter, rounder face and smaller ears than mice.

Habitat Very widespread, but primarily found in woodlands, hedgerows, park, and gardens.

Feeding Primary food is fruit, nuts, seeds, and buds early in the season. Often seen climbing among brambles looking for ripe fruits to collect. Also eats small insects. Very active and agile, often seen on bird tables and on the ground.

Plants Brambles where blackberries are plentiful; will feed on the seeds of a huge variety of shrubs and trees, including hazel and oak.

Breeding Female has 3 or 4 litters a year, each with 3 to 5 young. Does not hibernate. Typical lifespan is 6 months to a year.

FIELD VOLE
Microtus agrestis

Size Body: 8–13cm (3–5in) long; tail: 3–4cm (1¼–1½in).

ID features Grey-brown, with a pale grey colour on the underbelly, it has a shaggier appearance than bank vole. Sometimes known as the short-tailed vole. Active throughout the day and night.

Habitat Often hidden among vegetation on grassland, heathland, and moorland, and not as easily spotted as bank vole. Digs its tunnels under areas of long, rough grass, and moves along runways it creates within the grass, above the ground.

Feeding Mainly on seeds, roots, bark, and leaves. Can also be seen under feeders and will use small mammal feeders especially with tunnels.

Plants Likes dense vegetation especially when creating tunnel systems; benefits from having dense coverage such as bramble and gorse.

Breeding Female has 3 to 6 litters, each with 6 or 7 young, although numbers can fluctuate from one year to the next. It's thought that owls may reduce the numbers of voles one year, then the owls reduce too as they have fewer prey, then the voles breed again in larger numbers. Typical lifespan is 1 year.

COMMON SHREW
Sorex araneus

Size Body: 5–9cm (2–3½in) long; tail: 3–6cm (1¼–2½in).

ID features Dark brown fur on the back, reddish-chestnut sides, and a white tint on the underbelly – their fur is almost like velvet in texture. Long, pointed nose, very small ears hidden within fur.

Habitat Primarily found in grassland and at the edges of scrub, deciduous woodlands, grasslands, mixed woodlands, and arable fields. Also found in urban habitats including gardens.

Feeding Eats mainly invertebrates, especially worms and molluscs, woodlice, and ground-dwelling insects. Must eat every 2 to 3 hours to survive. Prey of many species such as tawny owl, weasel, fox, and kestrel, but often abandoned by the predator as it produces a foul-tasting liquid from its glands.

Plants Seeks dense vegetation with damp soil to create burrows, and uses those of other small mammals. Creates runs at the base of dense vegetation above ground.

Breeding Female has 3 to 4 litters of 5 to 7 young between May and September; these litters may have several fathers. It is possible to see a "caravan" of shrews running through your garden with young holding onto each other's trails in a chain after their mother. Does not hibernate but becomes much less active; shrinks in size in the winter so needs less energy to move around. Typical lifespan is 6 to 12 months.

Long whiskers on pointed nose

PYGMY SHREW
Sorex minutus

Size Body: 4–6cm (1½–2½in) long; tail: 3–4cm (1¼–1½in) long.

ID features Very small with greyish-brown fur over the back, head, and sides, and no distinct flank colour, unlike the common shrew. Proportionately, the tail is longer and thicker than that of common shrew. Long, pointed nose, very small eyes and ears.

Habitat Primarily found in grassland and near areas of scrub, woodlands, grasslands, and arable fields. Also found in gardens.

Feeding Insects, spiders, and woodlice; eats up to 125 per cent of its body weight in food each day. Produces a foul-tasting liquid from its glands when caught to deter predators.

Plants Create burrows underground, and runs above ground under dense vegetation.

Breeding Breeds between April and October, producing 2 or 3 litters of 5 to 7 young. Does not hibernate but becomes much less active; shrinks in size in the winter so needs less energy to move around. Typical lifespan is 6 to 12 months.

White underbelly

RED SQUIRREL
Sciurus vulgaris

Size Body: 18–20cm (7–8in) long; tail: 15–20cm (6–8in) long.

ID features Fur often bright ginger, red, or dark red with tints of grey and black during the winter months. The underparts are white. Long, fluffy red tail, and distinctive ear tufts. Much smaller than grey squirrel, with a daintier structure and a smaller head and face.

Habitat Mainly found among trees and hedges; commonly seen in coniferous and broadleaf woodlands.

Feeding Most of the diet is tree based, including tree seeds, tree flowers, and shoots. Also eats other woodland food such as fungi. May suffer food shortages during high summer months. Will take from squirrel feeders and peanut feeders.

Plants Hazel for its nuts, and conifers, especially Scots pine, for the seeds within the cones.

Breeding Begins around midwinter and can continue through the summer months depending on availability of feed. Female is able to breed from 1 year old, and has 1 or 2 litters a year, producing 2 or 3 young in each litter. Breeding takes place in a drey about two-thirds of the way up a conifer next to the trunk, or in holes in trees. Uses twigs and leaves to create the ball-shaped drey, and line it with soft hair, moss, and dried grass. Several red squirrels in the same family may share a drey. Will use a red squirrel box. Lifespan around 3 years.

GREY SQUIRREL
Sciurus carolinensis

Size Body: 24–28cm (9½–11in) long; tail: 19–24cm (7½–9½in).

ID features Mottled silver-grey/brown fur with browner fur on feet and face. Long, fluffy tail is fringed with brown and white. Much larger than red squirrel.

Habitat Found in a variety of different habitats, primarily natural woodlands, urban areas, and gardens.

Feeding Seeds of trees, flower buds, pine cones, fungi, sometimes bird eggs and chicks. Commonly seen around bird feeders and using squirrel feeders in gardens. Will also eat peanuts from garden feeders. Often creates caches of food to survive the autumn and winter months.

Plants Relies upon tree seeds such as those of oak, beech, hazel, sweet chestnut, and walnut.

Breeding Female is able to breed from 1 year old, and can have 2 litters of 3 or 4 young per year. Creates a drey high up in trees by collecting twigs and moss to make a spherical shape in which to breed. Typical lifespan of female is up to 5 years, male 2 to 3 years.

Brown tail ......

WEASEL
Mustela nivalis

Size Body: male 19–21cm (7½–8¼in), female 17–18cm (6¾–7in) long; tail: male 4–5cm (1½–2in), female 3–4cm (1¼–1½in).

ID features Long, sinuous body, ginger to light brown with a white belly, and a completely brown tail with no black tip. Short legs. Face is slightly pointed with rounded ears. Male is larger than female so they can be told apart if both are seen together. Both are smaller than stoats. It's the world's smallest carnivore.

Habitat Can use a variety of different habitats but primarily found in grasslands, arable land, woodland, and occasionally in urban habitats such as gardens and parks.

Feeding Very skilled in hunting small rodents such as mice, voles, and shrews and will occasionally hunt water voles too – with its small size and slender build, it's great at running through tunnels and along pathways made by different small mammals. Also eats small birds, eggs, and young rabbits.

Plants Uses vegetation as cover for hunting. Lines its burrow with leaves and moss to retain heat.

Breeding Typically has 1 litter of 4 to 6 young each year, but can have a second litter if food is abundant. Does not hibernate and is known to hunt in burrows under the snow. Lifespan is 1 to 2 years.

STOAT
Mustela erminea

Size Body: male 27–31cm (10½–12in), female 25–29cm (10–11½in) long; tail: 9–14cm (3½–5½in).

ID features Very long, slim body with short legs. Fur ginger to reddish-brown above with white below, a straight, clear line separating the two colours. Tail is bushier than that of a weasel and has a prominent black tip. Some animals have an "ermine" appearance in winter where their fur turns white or partially white.

Habitat Can be seen in a range of habitats, including deciduous woodlands, grasslands, heathlands, and arable land. Occasionally seen in urban areas and gardens.

Feeding Other small mammals, especially rabbits, but will also take mice, voles, and shrews. Feeds on birds, eggs, fruit, and even earthworms if other food is scarce.

Plants Relies upon low, dense vegetation for cover when hunting.

Breeding Female mates in early summer although does not give birth until the following spring when 1 large litter of 6 to 12 young is born. Maximum lifespan is around 5 years, although typically most animals only live 2 to 3 years.

White
...... underside

HEDGEHOG
Erinaceus europaeus

Size Body: 20–30cm (8–12in) long; tail: 2cm (¾in).

ID features Unmistakable due to the thousands of spines along its back, neck, and sides which are mottled brown, grey, and black. Face has a long, pointed nose, with plenty of fur, and small black eyes. Short tail.

Habitat Around mixed woodlands, heathland, and arable land. Often seen in urban areas and gardens if they have access points.

Feeding Beetles, worms, caterpillars, slugs, and other smaller invertebrates. May sometimes take eggs and chicks of ground-nesting birds. In autumn, eats fungi and soft fruits.

Plants Rests under the cover of plants during the day. Uses large, dense shrubs such as laurel hedges, bramble, and gorse as shelter under which to create a hibernation nest in autumn and winter.

Breeding Female has a litter of 4 or 5 young between April and September. May have a second litter, but offspring are often too small to survive hibernation. Hibernates between November and March, in a nest made of leaves typically under a bush, in a log pile or garden shed; will also use hedgehog homes and purpose-built hibernacula. Lifespan typically between 2 and 4 years, although many die within their first year.

MOLE
Talpa europaea

Size Body: 11–15cm (4½–6in) long; tail: 3–4cm (1¼–1½in).

ID features Very dark grey, velvet-like fur with pink feet and a pink nose. Eyes are minute and ears are not visible. Low to the ground, with short limbs; front feet are shaped like a spade for digging through the soil. Makes "mole hills" of earth from its burrowing – these are easier to see than the mole itself.

Habitat Grassland, arable land, woodlands, and urban areas, including gardens.

Feeding Mostly earthworms; needs to eat about its own weight in earthworms each day. Also eats insect larvae, particularly during summer months. Moles are prey to many species such as buzzards, tawny owls, and garden cats.

Plants Relies on good soil as it spends much of its life underground in a system of tunnels ranging from shallow ones near the surface to look for food and deep ones, which are used when soil is dry. Uses dry plant material such as hay and grass in its nest.

Breeding Female constructs a nest chamber among the tunnel systems, where she nests and raises her young; a litter of 3 or 4 young are born in the spring. Typical lifespan is around 3 years but some can live up to 6 years.

RABBIT
Oryctolagus cuniculus

Size Body: 30–40cm (12–16in) long; tail: 4–6cm (1½–2½in).

ID features Long ears and long hind legs; fur is a sandy/grey colour, with a fluffy tail that is white on the underside. Rounded face compared to hares.

Habitat A range of habitats, including grasslands, arable land, woodland edge, and in urban areas.

Feeding Herbivores, mainly eating plant material. Passes food through its system twice by eating own faeces in order to digest it fully.

Plants Grasses, cereal crops, and root vegetables; will occasionally eat small weeds and tree saplings. Uses dense vegetation to hide among, only stepping out a few feet to feed; often seen around gorse, bramble, wild rose, and other shrub-like plants where they can create a burrow.

Breeding Between January and August, providing 3 to 7 kits per month. Burrows through sand and soil, creating a communal warren in which the females make nesting chambers, lined with their own fur. Lifespan around 3 years, although many die within the first year, often from disease.

Black ear tip

BROWN HARE
Lepus europaeus

Size Body: 50–70cm (20–28in) long; tail: 7–10cm (2¾–4in).

ID features Brown with some black streaks in the fur; ears are long and tipped black. Hind legs are long and powerful; often seen standing rather than hunched like a rabbit. Looks similar to a rabbit but much larger.

Habitat Grassland and arable land, often in woodland. May enter large gardens in agricultural settings.

Feeding Tender grass shoots; will pull plants from the ground to munch on. Passes food through its system twice by eating own faeces in order to digest it fully.

Plants Wild grasses and cereal crops such as maize, barley, and rapeseed. Hares also use these plants to hide among, their dusky fur providing camouflage. Leverets (young hares) hide among tussocks of grass while the female ventures out to feed.

Breeding Between February and September, with females having 3 or 4 litters a year, with 2 or 3 young in each litter. Can be seen boxing during the early spring months: males pursue females, and the female turns and lashes out at the male if she wants him to leave. Typical lifespan is between 3 and 4 years.

Dense, brown fur

SOPRANO PIPISTRELLE
Pipistrellus pygmaeus

Size 3–5cm long (1¼–2in); wingspan: 20cm (8in).

ID features Small bat with medium-brown fur, rounded nose shape, and short, blunt ears. Looks very similar to common pipistrelle. Peak call frequency is 55kHz.

Habitat Woodlands and urban and suburban areas, especially near lakes and rivers.

Feeding Emerges early from roosts to feed before dusk has set in. Feeds mid-level below the canopy, often over water, looking for small moths, midges, and other nocturnal flying insects.

Plants Stays below canopy level although will use trees to navigate throughout gardens. Can use tree crevices to create a roost, although preference is for buildings, barns, and churches.

Breeding Mates in late summer to early autumn. Female joins a maternity colony in spring and gives birth to 1 pup in midsummer. Summer roosts mostly in buildings, winter roosts in buildings or crevices in trees; takes readily to bat boxes. Hibernates in winter. Typical lifespan is 4 to 5 years, although some have been recorded up to 15 years old.

COMMON PIPISTRELLE
Pipistrellus pipistrellus

Size 3–5cm (1¼–2in) long; wingspan: 20cm (8in).

ID features Small bat with medium-brown fur, rounded nose shape, and short, blunt ears. Peak call frequency is 45kHz.

Habitat Grasslands, urban and suburban gardens, woodlands, heathlands, and often over water.

Feeding Emerges early from roosts to feed before dusk has set in. Feeds at mid-level below the canopy looking for small moths, midges, and other nocturnal flying insects.

Plants Stays below canopy level although will use trees to navigate throughout gardens. Can use tree crevices to create a roost, although prefers buildings, barns, and churches.

Breeding Mating takes place in autumn and winter, but female gives birth to 1 pup the following summer in a maternity colony. These colonies of females are large, very noisy and active, and can include several hundred bats. These roosts are prime locations to see common pipistrelles emerging from buildings. Takes readily to bat boxes. Hibernates in winter. Typical lifespan is 4 to 5 years although some have been recorded up to 16 years.

Rounded nose

NOCTULE
Nyctalus noctula

Size Large; 6–9cm (2–3in) long; wingspan: 40–45cm (16–18in).

ID features Large bat with bright ginger, glossy fur, which turns duller after its summer moult. Ears are rounded and the tragus (flap of skin in the ear) is mushroom-shaped. Its muzzle is dark brown. Has a double "chip-chop" call at peak frequency of 25 and 19kHz respectively.

Habitat Broadleaf woodlands, open areas of grassland and wetlands. Can also be seen over ponds and rivers.

Feeding Feeds on a wide diet of insects including large beetles, flies, and moths. Feeds up high at the top of tree canopies and well above, sometimes up ot 50m (165ft) high over open ground. Often the first bat to leave its roost well before sunset, flying straight out to its foraging grounds.

Plants Flies above canopy level using tops of trees to navigate. Uses tree holes to roost in; a few individuals may use one tree.

Breeding Mating takes place at the end of summer. Females form maternity roosts in spring, and each gives birth to 1 pup in midsummer. Typical lifespan is 10 to 12 years.

DAUBENTON'S BAT
Myotis daubentonii

Size 4cm (1½in) long; wingspan: 25cm (10in).

ID features Medium-sized bat with short ears. Its fur is brown on its back and whitish on the underbelly. Peak call frequency is 47kHz. Has a steady, less jerky flight than other bats that fly over water.

Habitat Found in broadleaf woodland and most commonly seen flying to feed over water.

Feeding Feeds over water bodies, looking for insects such as mayflies and midges, which it will take from just above or on the water surface. Emerges to feed late, typically an hour after sunset.

Plants Navigates water sources using vegetation, especially hedges, around the location; summer roosts are primarily in trees in woodlands.

Breeding Mating takes place in autumn. Female joins a maternity roost in spring, often in trees of broadleaf woodlands although they are known to roost in solitary trees, bat boxes on trees without natural crevices, and under bridges. Gives birth to 1 pup in spring or summer. Typical lifespan is 4 to 5 years, but some live for more than 20 years.

White underside

WHISKERED BAT
Myotis mystacinus

Size 3–5cm (1¼–2in) long; wingspan: 20–25cm (8–10in).

ID features Small bat with dark grey, shaggy fur, and very dark face and wing membranes. Has long, pointed ears, and rounded nose. Peak call frequency is between 53 and 60kHz.

Habitat Primarily found in woodlands, orchards, grasslands, as well as over hedgerows and scrubland.

Feeding A hawking bat, chasing after its prey through the air with a fluttering, butterfly-like flight. Feeds mainly on small moths and flies.

Plants Uses large linear vegetation features, such as woodland edges or hedgerows, to help in navigating. Agile flyer within orchards and woodlands.

Breeding Mating takes place in autumn. Maternity roosts are often in buildings, although also in trees and bat boxes. Female gives birth to 1 pup in spring. Typical lifespan is 4 to 5 years, although some have reached over 10 years. Winter roost underground in caves, tunnels, and cellars. In autumn forms swarms around the mouth of hibernation locations.

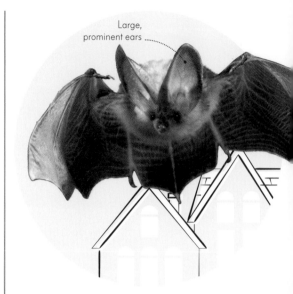

Large, prominent ears

BROWN LONG-EARED BAT
Plecotus auritus

Size 4–6cm (1½–2½in) long; wingspan: 20–30cm (8–12in).

ID features Small bat with medium brown fur, and very long, big ears. Peak call frequency is 35kHz, but echolocation calls are very quiet and barely discernible even with a bat detector.

Habitat Mainly deciduous and mixed woodlands, also parks and gardens.

Feeding Small moths, beetles, and flies taken by hawking and gleaning its prey off foliage, the bat hovering close to the leaves.

Plants Will occasionally use tree crevices as a place to roost in summer and winter.

Breeding Mating takes place in the autumn; female joins the maternity roosts in spring, giving birth in midsummer. Summer roosts are often in buildings and sometimes bat boxes; winter roosts are mostly underground in cellars, tunnels, and caves. Typical lifespan is 4 to 5 years.

LESSER HORSESHOE BAT
Rhinolophus hipposideros

Size 3–5cm (1¼–2in) long; wingspan 19–25cm (7½–10in).

ID features Small bat with light brown fur, rounded ears, and characteristic horseshoe nose shape. Peak call frequency is 110kHz.

Habitat Found in Wales and southwest England in deciduous woodlands, hedgerows, scrubland, and over pasture.

Feeding Feeds on small flies and moths by hawking (chasing its prey on the wing) and gleaning (taking the prey from a surface such as a leaf), usually flying low over the ground.

Plants Relies upon hedgerows and tree lines for cover whilst travelling between roosts and feeding grounds.

Breeding Mating takes place in autumn, with females forming roosts in spring, often in the roof of old, spacious buildings such as churches and barns. Female gives birth in July to 1 pup. Winter roosts are underground. Will take to bat racks in buildings or sheds. Lives for up to 20 years.

Horseshoe-shaped nose

GREATER HORSESHOE BAT
Rhinolophus ferrumequinum

Size 5–7cm (2–2¾in) long; wingspan: 40cm (16in).

ID features Large bat with light brown fur, long ears, and characteristic horseshoe nose shape. Peak call frequency is 82kHz.

Habitat Found in woodlands and pastures in the southwest of England.

Feeding Large insects such as beetles and moths.

Plants Relies upon hedgerows to navigate whilst travelling between feeding and roosting grounds.

Breeding Mating takes place in autumn, and mating roosts are often in underground areas such as small caves, tunnels, and cellars of old buildings; these roosts are primarily made up of a few individuals. Maternity colonies form in the roof spaces of old buildings in late spring and female give birth to 1 pup in midsummer; she does this while hanging upside down. Winter roosts are underground in caves or mines. Will take to bat racks in buildings or sheds. The longest-lived British bat, it can live up to 30 years.

FOX
Vulpes vulpes

Size Body: male 67–90cm (27–36in), female 62–67cm (25–27in); tail around 40cm (16in).

ID features Dog-like, with reddish-orange fur, white on the underbelly and sides, and brown-black socks on the feet. Has black-tipped ears. Unmistakable bushy tail, bright orange with black fringes.

Habitat Found in a very wide variety of habitats: towns and cities, gardens, rivers and wetlands, marshland, and woodlands. Mainly active at dawn and dusk, but can be seen in the day, especially in urban areas.

Feeding Omnivorous with a varied diet, depending on its habitat. In countryside may eat mice, voles, shrews, rabbits, beetles, and fruit – and perhaps the odd bird. An urban fox scavenges through dustbins, under bird tables, and from compost heaps. A coastal fox may eat crabs and dead seabirds.

Plants May create a den at the base of shrubs and tree roots; low-down parted vegetation may indicate a fox route through the garden.

Breeding Foxes move around in a family group, usually consisting of a dog fox and vixen and their cubs. Each family has a territory; these are rarely shared unless food is plentiful, such as in urban environments. Their den may be in an old rabbit burrow, under shrubs and trees, or in cities they may use the underneath of sheds or compost heaps as the soil is softer. Vixen produces a litter of 4 or 5 cubs. Lifespan can vary but average is between 1 and 4 years, with some records show individuals living to 10 years.

BADGER
Meles meles

Size Body: 60–90cm (24–36in) long; tail: 15cm (6in).

ID features Long, pointed face with distinctive black stripes over the eyes and down the snout and white stripe at the centre and edges. Body fur is grey with mottled brown appearance and black fur on the legs. Often low to the ground and heard before it is seen: listen out for snuffling!

Habitat Primarily found in woodlands. Can also be seen in urban environments such as gardens and parks. Nocturnal, and rarely seen in the day, instead spending much of its time in its sett – a network of tunnels that may have been used for several generations. Family groups, known as clans, emerge at dusk to head out on their feeding trip, often on grassland or garden lawns.

Feeding Feeds on creatures within the soil, particularly earthworms, but also slugs, beetle larvae, and bees and wasps after demolishing their nests. Will also eat fruits and berries.

Plants Setts are often located at the base of large trees such as sycamore and oak. Hawthorn, blackthorn, and bramble provide berries.

Breeding Mating takes place between February and May, and the litter of 2 or 3 cubs is born the following January or February. Usually only 1 female in each group has cubs, but sometimes 2 or 3 females reproduce (a clan can have up to 20 adults, although most contain around 5 to 7). Life expectancy is around 14 years, although many do not live that long due to traffic collisions among a number of other threats.

Large paws and claws ⋯⋯

Small ears

OTTER
Lutra lutra

Size Body: 60–80cm (24–32in) long; tail: 32–56cm (13–22in).

ID features Brown fur, with paler fur under the belly and neck; long, slender body. Small ears on a broad head. Very thick tail, ideal for swimming. In the water swims very low with just a head and some of the back showing. Male is a much heavier build than female.

Habitat Found in rivers, wetlands, and coastal marshes. As the population has grown over the last three decades, they have moved into more urban water bodies.

Feeding Primarily fish and eels, and will eat crayfish too. River and pond otters will take frogs and toads out of the water to feed upon. Also known to eat water birds and small mammals.

Plants Creates a den known as a holt in the base of tree root systems, holes in the bank, or under a pile of rocks. Does not feed on plants but can be tracked through its preferred areas by looking for large tunnels among vegetation around water sources.

Breeding Female has 2 or 3 cubs per year, raising them in her holt. Can live up to 10 years, although many live shorter lives.

PINE MARTEN
Martes martes

Size Body: male 51–54cm (20–21in), female 35–45cm (14–18in); tail: male 26–28cm (10¼–11in), female 18–24cm (7–9½in).

ID features Dark, rich brown fur with a yellowish throat patch. Rounded ears. The tail is long and fluffy, similar to that of a cat. Males are larger than females with a longer tail.

Habitat Primarily coniferous woodland, but also deciduous and mixed. Will visit gardens that are in the remote landscapes that it favours.

Feeding Omnivorous predator, feeding on small rodents such as mice and voles, but also birds, beetles, carrion, and fungi – and has a preference for eggs. In autumn, will feed on berries. Scavenges from bird tables and bins.

Plants Makes its den in cavities in hollow trees or among the roots of pine trees and other large conifers.

Breeding Female has 1 litter of 1 to 5 kits in early spring. Males do not play any direct part in rearing the young. If suitable trees are not available for its den, may use rocks covered with scrub, or buildings such as outhouses. Lifespan of up to 8 years.

OBSERVING
GARDEN
WILDLIFE

OBSERVING GARDEN WILDLIFE

As you create a wilder garden, you will come to notice more about the creatures that visit your patch. There are plenty of ways to enrich your experience of the nature in your garden, from looking for tracks and traces, to photographing or filming species as they pass through, or raise their young. You may also want to share your enthusiasm with others, and expand your own wildlife horizons at the same time by joining wildlife groups and activities.

Some species come back time and again to a favourite garden spot, offering a change to observe them closely.

WILDLIFE TRACKING

As you attract more wildlife, you can learn to spot clues that different visitors have stopped by, so that you can better cater for their needs.

While there are a number of more technical ways to observe garden visitors (see pp.180–81), it's worth getting to know some of the "old school" techniques: identifying footprints, droppings, and other traces. These are ways to get to know the visiting wildlife without disturbing them, and they also enable you to test your observation skills.

Footprints

It's easiest to see footprints in damp mud or sand, and in snowy conditions, rather than on dry soil and in areas of vegetation, so winter is an ideal time to start tracking. You can practise your identification skills in a local reserve or park as well as in your garden. Making a tracking

pad is a way to obtain footprints in your garden to observe up close (see pp.156–57).

When looking at footprints, we need to first imagine how an animal may be travelling. What sort of distance is between prints? Is it possible to work out a stride pattern? A fox, for instance, has a large stride compared to other mammals, of up to 30cm (12in), so we expect to see one footprint with another further up the track, whereas an otter has a short stride, and would have with an unmistakable tail drag behind the footprints. Some animals such as frogs or rabbits jump, leaving a pair of prints.

Mammals mostly have a larger central rear pad and several toe pads; some have visible claw marks. Within each type of print, it becomes harder to narrow down to a species, especially for groups such as mice where there is little variety in the foot structure and stride. Prints of perching birds have three toes forward and one toe back. Frogs and toads have sticky toes, which form little bloba on the end of their feet, so spotting these in wet mud is relatively easy.

Brown hares have a distinctive gait, bounding along with hind legs parallel.

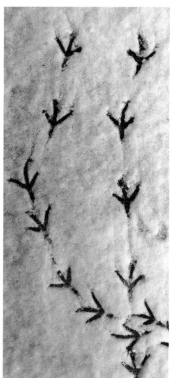

Impressions

Clockwise from top: badgers are large so make deep indentations; woodpigeons make firm prints as they waddle; weasel prints are light and hand-shaped; hare prints show two larger hind prints together, and the front paws stepping forward.

Chew and bite marks

We can also look at different natural food sources and notice nibble and chew marks to help us identify which species are visiting the garden, even if we can't see them on the plants. Invertebrates such as slugs and snails may consume whole leaves, but smaller species such as caterpillars and leaf-cutter bees partially remove the leaves. Many animals eat berries whole, but it's possible to see marks of beaks or teeth chew marks on larger fruits. Nuts take time to extract, so there are often teeth marks of mice or squirrels on the shell.

Chew marks
Caterpillars eat holes in and around leaves of their foodplant. In some cases, they can strip the leaves.

Droppings and pellets

It might seem unpleasant to study what animals leave behind, but droppings and pellets can tell us a lot. Looking at droppings, or latrines (wildlife toilet areas where species habitually urinate and leave droppings) allows us to observe what wildlife has been attracted to our space.

We can look for evidence of what the species has been eating and then use that to narrow down the identification. The surrounding habitat is also an important clue. Otters have a fish-based diet, so scales and small fish are likely to be present, along with a fishy smell. Badgers and foxes eat beetle larvae and berries, and the

remains of these can be seen in the latrines, often with a purple tint to the droppings. Mice are small and their droppings are small and pellet-shaped, found amid vegetation. Herbivore droppings are often drier and larger than carnivore droppings. Reptiles and amphibians don't tend to leave identifiable droppings.

Pellets are the undigested remains of food coughed up by some birds, especially owls and members of the crow family. It's possible to gently take apart these pellets, which are usually dry and don't smell, to identify what the bird has eaten. Bones can often be seen in owl pellets.

Beak holes
Birds make holes in fruit using their beaks. These holes are prone to rot and other infections.

Signs of gnawing
Squirrel bite marks range from tooth marks on the outside to splittingthe nut in half.

Droppings
Rabbit droppings, like those of other herbivores, are small and round, consisting of undigested plant fibres. Droppings are found in latrines near burrow entrances.

Pellets
A raven or jackdaw pellet may contain indigestible parts of insects such as beetles, as well as seeds, fruit, and sometimes bones.

CAMERAS AND OBSERVATION

Wildlife cameras, including CCTV and night-vision systems, offer a valuable way to observe wildlife without disturbing their routines.

Cameras give us a unique insight into the lives of our garden visitors. There's nothing quite like the delight of playing back footage from a wildlife camera and seeing a creature return night after night, or watching them explore different areas of the garden when we aren't around. Many different kinds of cameras are sold; here are just a few you might want to try.

Camera trap

A standard item in many ecologists' kit, the camera trap, also known as a trail camera, is invaluable to observe wildlife – day and night. The camera is placed in a location where wildlife is likely to pass by. Motion or heat detectors ensure that the camera is triggered when an animal passes. When choosing a camera, ensure it is waterproof, and can take images of a good enough resolution to allow you to identify smaller species.

Nest box with camera

Camera trap attached low down on a tree.

Nest-box cameras offer a close-up, 24-hour view inside the box without disturbing the wildlife. You can watch animals and birds sheltering, hibernating, or even raising their young.

Nest-box cameras

These are a great way to get more out of the work that you have done to attract more species to your garden. Nest-box cameras are small enough to install into an existing nest or shelter box. Choose a time out of the busy breeding, nesting, or hibernation seasons, when the box is deserted, to install the camera. Once the box is occupied, plug in the camera to power it and watch live on your computer or device. There are different models such as Wi-Fi cameras, wired cameras, and completely wireless versions. It's also possible to purchase a new nest box with a camera already fitted.

AI technology

An AI-equipped camera trap identifies the wildlife in the images it records, and notifies you via an app. There are different models and, as you might expect, they come with quite a price tag. However, they can be brilliant for showing you wildlife up close. For example, a camera monitoring bird feeders would send a notification of which species are there at that moment.

COMMUNITY WILDLIFE WATCHING

Wildlife watching can sometimes feel like a solitary hobby, but it's worth looking to see if you can find and join a community that shares your enthusiasm.

There are many ways to get involved with wildlife groups and meet people in real life or online who find wildlife as fascinating as you do. You can share your experiences of changing your garden to attract wildlife, and find out things that have worked for others – or gain an insight into completely different species and habitats.

Community groups

Many areas have groups that share your enthusiasm for wildlife, including local bird clubs and natural history groups. Nature reserves often have conservation groups that you can join in with. Look out for posters in your local library, through community social media pages, or search for your local Wildlife Trust. There may be talks from local experts during the winter, and guided walks or events at nature reserves in the summer. These are great for making contacts in your area and getting to know its wildlife in depth.

Local events

Something that I absolutely love and find hugely rewarding is running and attending local events.

There are several wildlife themed weeks and days across the year such as Moth Night, International Dawn Chorus Day, and Mammal Awareness Week that all deserve attention. You can join in by running an event in your local park, getting your street involved, or attending a local event hosted by a wildlife community group.

Social media groups

In addition to local community groups, social media is a brilliant way of connecting with like-minded wildlife lovers. You'll find plenty of Twitter accounts that post regular wildlife content, Instagram is a hub for photography and engaging stories, and Facebook has countless wildlife groups that share images, news, and dates of events. You can follow the accounts that interest you, and interact, asking questions and sharing your experience. Often the groups specialize in certain wildlife and are a great source of knowledge, where people post their first sightings of migrant birds or unusual species. If you're not sure where to start, you can always find me on Twitter or Instagram @DanERouse.

Wildlife watching in a group offers opportunities to share knowledge and tips on identification and equipment. Local events can be a way of getting everyone involved and spreading enthusiasm for wildlife through the community.

PLANT DIRECTORY

No matter what kind of garden you have,
you can make it more wildlife-friendly
by adding the right kind of plants.

Here is just a small selection of plants that support garden wildlife. Many are excellent sources of food for pollinators, birds, and small mammals, while others provide shelter. Opposite, you'll find ten particularly great plants that offer a variety of wildlife benefits. For more inspiration, visit a local RHS or National Trust garden and let nature show you what it loves.

Planting for pollinators
(* indicates night-flowering plant)
Early flowering:
- Common cowslip (*Primula veris*)
- Meadow cranesbill (*Geranium pratense*)
- Gorse (*Ulex europaeus*)
- Moss phlox* (*Phlox subulata*)

Mid-flowering:
- Dandelion (*Taraxacum officinale*)
- Allium (*Allium* spp.)
- Sweet pea (*Lathyrus odoratus*)
- Cocksfoot (*Dactylis glomerata*)
- Heather* (*Calluna vulgaris*)
- Foxglove (*Digitalis purpurea*)
- Oregano (*Origanum vulgare*)
- Borage (*Borago officinalis*)
- Fennel (*Foeniculum vulgare*)
- Evening primrose* (*Oenothera biennis*)

Late-flowering:
- Michaelmas daisy (*Aster × frikartii* 'Mönch')
- Purple verbena (*Verbena bonariensis*)
- Buddleia (*Buddleja davidii*)
- Sedum (*Sedum* spp.)

- Mahonia (*Mahonia* spp.)
- Hellebore (*Helleborus* spp.)
- Laurustinus (*Viburnum tinus*)

Planting for seeds
- Spear thistle (*Cirsium vulgare*)
- Common poppy (*Papaver rhoeas*)
- Teasel (*Dipsacus fullonum*)
- Alexanders (*Smyrnium olusatrum*)

Planting for fruit or nuts
- Cherry (*Prunus* spp.)
- Apple (*Malus* spp.)
- Hazel (*Corylus avellana*)
- Oak (*Quercus robur*)
- Sweet chestnut (*Castanea sativa*)

Planting for berries
- Blackthorn (*Prunus spinosa*)
- Hawthorn (*Crataegus* spp.)
- Elder (*Sambucus nigra*)
- Cotoneaster (*Cotoneaster horizontalis*)
- Firethorn (*Pyracantha coccinea*)
- Sea buckthorn (*Hippophae rhamnoides*)

Plants for shelter
- Spotted laurel (*Aucuba* spp.)
- Gorse (*Ulex europaeus*)
- Wild privet (*Ligustrum vulgare*)
- Juniper (*Juniperus communis*)
- Bay (*Laurus nobilis*)

Plants for containers
- Fuchsia (*Fuchsia* spp.)
- Cyclamen (*Cyclamen hederifolium*)
- Pansy (*Viola* spp.)
- Petunia (*Petunia* spp.)
- Busy Lizzie (*Impatiens* spp.)
- Geranium (*Geranium* spp.)
- Cosmos (*Cosmos bipinnatus*)
- Poached-egg plant (*Limnanthes douglasii*)

Plants for meadows
- Oxeye daisy (*Leucanthemum vulgare*)
- Viper's bugloss (*Echium vulgare*)
- Common knapweed (*Centaurea nigra*)

Plant name	Description	Flowers	Other benefits
English lavender *Lavandula angustifolia*	• Evergreen shrub, up to 1m (3ft) tall • Full sun • Well-drained soil	• Summer- to autumn-flowering • Heavily scented • Pollen-rich	• Reptiles use bare stems for shelter • Insects hide among the twiggy stems
Nettle *Urtica dioica*	• Perennial wildflower, up to 2m (6½ft) tall • Any sun/soil conditions	• Summer- to autumn-flowering • Pollen-rich	• Caterpillar foodplant • Lots of cover for small creatures moving about
Nasturtium *Tropaeolum majus*	• Annual climber, up to 2.5m (8ft) tall • Full sun; well-drained soil	• Summer- to autumn-flowering • Pollen-rich	• Caterpillar foodplant • Leaves gather water, which invertebrates can drink
Ivy *Hedera* spp.	• Evergreen climber, up to 10m (33ft) tall • Any sun/soil conditions; a great choice for shady areas and small gardens	• Autumn-flowering • Pollen-rich • Flower buds are a foodplant for holly blue butterflies	• Winter berries provide an essential food source for birds when other sources are scarce • Lots of cover for small creatures moving about
Sunflower *Helianthus annuus*	• Annual, up to 4m (13ft) tall • Full sun; moist but well-drained soil	• Summer-flowering • Pollen-rich • Seeds for birds in late summer	• Large stems are a favourite for hares and badgers to munch on
Holly *Ilex aquifolium*	• Evergreen shrub/tree, up to 12m (39ft) tall but often shorter • Full sun/partial shade; Moist, well-drained soil	• Spring- to summer-flowering; also night-flowering • Pollen-rich	• Berries in autumn and winter • Provides great year-round shelter, especially in winter when shelter may be scarce
Honeysuckle *Lonicera* spp.	• Annual climber, up to 8m (26ft) • Full sun/partial shade; well-drained soil	• Summer- to autumn-flowering • Pollen-rich • Heavily scented	• Cover for nesting birds • Mice use shreds of its papery bark to line their nests
Red valerian *Centranthus ruber*	• Annual, up to 80cm (32in) tall • Full sun; well-drained chalky or stony soil	• Summer-flowering • Pollen-rich	• Favourite plant of hummingbird hawkmoths • Great cover for small creatures moving about
Yellow rattle *Rhinanthus minor*	• Annual, up to 30cm (12in) tall • Full sun; well-drained soil	• Summer-flowering • Pollen-rich	• Helps turn grassy lawns into meadows by suppressing grass growth with its parasitic action
Silver birch *Betula pendula*	• Deciduous tree, up to 12m (39ft) tall • Any sun/soil conditions	• Spring-flowering • Pollen-rich	• Loose bark ideal where insects hibernate and breed

USEFUL RESOURCES

ADDITIONAL WILDLIFE AND GARDENING INFORMATION

Amphibian and Reptile Conservation (ARC)
Specialist information on reptiles and amphibians.
arc-trust.org

British Trust for Ornithology (BTO)
Information on birds and ornithology.
bto.org

Buglife
Information on insects and how to conserve them.
buglife.org.uk

Bumblebee Conservation Trust
Specialist information on bumblebees and other bees.
bumblebeeconservation.org

Butterfly Conservation
Specialist information on butterflies and moths.
butterfly-conservation.org

Royal Horticultural Society (RHS)
Information on plants both native and non-native, and on wildlife gardening.
rhs.org.uk/wildlife

Royal Society for the Protection of Birds (RSPB)
General bird information including gardening for birds, conservation, and research.
rspb.org.uk

Simon King
Online resource and shop for wildlife gardening.
simonkingwildlife.com

Wildlife Trusts
Support for nature, including garden wildlife information.wildlifetrusts.org

Wildlife World UK
Stockists of wildlife gardening products.
wildlifeworld.co.uk

Woodland Trust
Information on habitats, wildlife, and trees.
woodlandtrust.org.uk

BOOKS AND PUBLICATIONS

How to Attract Birds to Your Garden
Dan Rouse's first guide to garden wildlife, published by DK (2020).

No Dig
An essential guide to no-dig gardening principles from expert Charles Dowding, published by DK (2022).

Bloomsbury Field Guides
Comprehensive guides to different kinds of wildlife found in Great Britain and Ireland.
bloomsbury.com/uk/series/bloomsbury-wildlife-guides

Field Study Council
Fold-out identification guides to groups of species.
field-studies-council.org

Pelagic Publishing
Specialist reading on ecology and wildlife.
pelagicpublishing.com

Princeton WILDGuides
A range of photographic guides.
press.princeton.edu/series/wildguides

INDEX

PICTURE CREDITS

The publisher would like to thank the following for their kind permission to reproduce their photographs:
(Key: a-above; b-below/bottom; c-centre; f-far; l-left; r-right; t-top)

DK LONDON

Project editor Amy Slack
Senior designer Louise Brigenshaw
Senior production editor Tony Phipps
Production controller Rebecca Parton
Jacket designer Amy Cox
Jacket co-ordinator Jasmin Lennie
Editorial manager Ruth O'Rourke
Design manager Marianne Markham
Art director Maxine Pedliham
Publishing director Katie Cowan

Editorial Jane Simmonds
Design Tom Forge, Emma Forge
Illustration Keith Hagan

First published in Great Britain in 2023 by
Dorling Kindersley Limited
DK, One Embassy Gardens, 8 Viaduct Gardens,
London, SW11 7BW

The authorised representative in the EEA is
Dorling Kindersley Verlag GmbH. Arnulfstr. 124,
80636 Munich, Germany

A CIP catalogue record for this book
is available from the British Library.
ISBN: 978-0-2415-9330-1

Printed and bound in China

For the curious
www.dk.com

About the author

Dan Rouse is a passionate wildlife conservationist and
ornithologist, and is the author of DK's *How to Attract Birds to
Your Garden*. She grew up on the South Wales coastline, where
she developed a passion for coastal birds and wildlife, and is
widely respected in the birding and Welsh communities for her
ornithological and conservation work. Dan has appeared on TV
shows including *Countryfile* (BBC 1), Iolo Williams' *Urban Nature*
(BBC 1) and *Coast & Country* (ITV), and has also appeared
regularly on BBC Radio Cymru, BBC Radio Wales, and BBC
Radio 4. She currently presents videos on wildlife and wildlife
science for S4C Hansh.

You can follow Dan online at:
Twitter: **@DanERouse**
Instagram: **@danerouse**
Youtube: **Dan Rouse**
Facebook: **facebook.com/DanERouseTV**
Website: **danrouse.org.uk**

Author acknowledgments

Never-ending love and thanks must go to my brother, James.
Growing up, we were always out in the garden exploring and
enjoying the wildlife. Now grown up, we continue to share our
love for our garden wildlife by creating online content together,
designing wildlife-friendly spaces in our gardens and beyond,
and generally spending time doing something we both love.

Additional thank-yous go to my father, my partner Sam who
always supports any endeavours I come up with, and to my mum
Jacqui and step-dad Chris (who now try to introduce wildlife to
their own gardens!) for their endless support.

Publisher acknowledgments

DK would like to thank Chris Gibson for consulting on this title. We
would also like to thank Aditya Katyal, Vagish Pushp, and Ahmed
Bilal Khan for picture research, Eloise Grohs for design assistance,
Francesco Piscitelli for proofreading, and Ruth Ellis for indexing.
Thank you to Wildlife World for use of images of their products.

MIX
Paper | Supporting
responsible forestry
FSC™ C018179

This book was made with Forest
Stewardship Council ™ certified
paper - one small step in DK's
commitment to a sustainable future.
For more information go to
www.dk.com/our-green-pledge